Live Like a Queen

REIGNING IN REAL LIFE

JEAN STOCKDALE

 CrossHouse

Published by
CrossHouse Publishing
PO Box 461592
Garland, TX 75046-1592
Copyright Jean Stockdale 2008
All Rights Reserved
Printed in the United States of America
by Lightning Source, LaVergne, TN
Cover design by Dennis Davidson
Except where otherwise indicated, all Scripture taken from the
NEW AMERICAN STANDARD BIBLE,
Copyright 1960, 1962, 1963, 1968, 1971, 1972, 1975, 1977,
by the Lockman Foundation. Used by permission.
ISBN 978-1-934749-27-2
Library of Congress Control Number: 2008932794

TO ORDER ADDITIONAL COPIES FOR $14.95 EACH (ADD $3.00 SHIPPING FOR FIRST BOOK,
$1.00 FOR EACH ADDITIONAL BOOK) CONTACT
CROSSHOUSE PUBLISHING
PO BOX 461592
GARLAND, TX 75046-1592
www.crosshousepublishing.com
877-212-0933 (toll free)

Dedication

This book is lovingly dedicated to my family. Without you,
I would not have a story to tell.

To my darling husband, Craig

Your devotion to the Lord Jesus Christ has driven me to become a student of the Word of God. Watching you develop a devotional love for the Lord has challenged my faith walk. I am grateful for your encouragement and support. Thank you for allowing me the luxury of spending countless hours at my computer to research and write. My passion for the things of God mirrors your own. I have consistently seen the reality of Christ in you. Your love for the Lord has compelled me to aggressively pursue personal holiness and practical righteousness in my own life. Being around you makes me want to become more like Jesus. God has allowed us to launch two fine men into the adult world. He has graced us with two precious daughters-in-law and some grandbabies.
I love you more than words can express.

To our guys and their girls, Jason and Patti, Dawson and Kathryn

Building your own households of faith is such a sweet delight. Craig and I are so proud of the godly adults you have become. I thank you for allowing me to instruct and encourage moms and to share personal illustrations from our lives. Letting others look inside the workings of our Christian home has been daunting at times, but God has used it to bless the hearts of many mommas.

To our grandsons, Declan and Grayson

You boys have made our lives exceedingly sweet. As you grow, I am confident your stories often will show up in my writing and teaching. You make my heart hurt with joy! Our prayer is that at an early age you will receive the Lord and will live for Him.
Poppa and I love you very much!

Acknowledgements

To My Extended Family

Thanks to my mom, **Ann Waters**, for all the encouraging words, time, energy, and love you have invested in my life. Without your strong support I would not have had the courage to undertake this project. I also want to honor the memory of my dad, **Harold Waters**, and my in-laws, **Bob and Frances Stockdale,** who are all safely home with the Lord.

To My Buddy, Renae Terrell

No one deserves to have a friend in the faith like you. As a co-laborer in the ministry, you are invaluable. Without your countless hours of diligent work and your limitless supply of encouragement, this project would not have happened. I rely on your creativity. I rest in your discretion. I value your insight. I admire your discernment. I trust your judgment. I value your friendship. Only eternity will reveal the many ways your fingerprints are on this work. Craig and I value the friendship we share with you and Roy and respect it as a gift from the Lord. I bless you and Roy in the name of the Lord Jesus Christ.

Contents

Foreword

Canvas or temple: your choice. Both are beautiful. The first fades, while the second endures. Like the masterful portraits capturing the beauty of Princess Diana, the first choice catches the sparkling crown of remembrance of a beautiful monarch of the past. The other choice . . . more difficult, to be sure . . . yet, to choose temple-life, is to step out of the halls of British monarchy and step into the pages of the Bible. A temple, with its interior beauty, more adequately captures the life of Queen Esther than that of a canvas, which captures only external beauty.

Had Esther chosen only to live the life of a beauty queen, this 17th book of the Bible would look quite different both in title and in content. Because Esther chose to be more than a canvas, we who study her life can see and experience God similarly.

To meet those who have sat under the teaching ministry of Jean Stockdale is to meet women more interested in being a temple than a canvas, having a life of content rather than a life of surface.

Like Esther of yesteryear God has raised up Jean Stockdale *for such a time as this.* Jean plows beneath the surface of the Book of Esther and brings the reader into the inner sanctuary of God's work in a world in which God's people needed rescuing. To study *Live Like a Queen* is to see God's redemptive activity in today's world in which we, too, need to be rescued from living lives of vanity while the world around us actively seeks to destroy our Christian voice. *Live Like a Queen* challenges every woman to live "for such a time as this."

Jean is a favored Bible teacher at Bellevue Baptist Church, where for 20 years she has faithfully entered the lives of younger women. To read her many books and to hear her teaching is to sit under a mature woman of wisdom and wit—and to experience temple-life.

Iva G. May, Author of *Shepherd-Shaped, I am My Beloved's and He is Mine*
and *W3: Women, Worldview, and the Word*

Opening Letter

My dear mommas,

You are about to embark on the study entitled *Live Like a Queen*, a study of the Book of Esther. I encourage you to apply yourself to the in-depth study of the Word of God. Be prepared to learn wonderful truths that will enrich your Christian life and enlarge your understanding of the things of God. Studying Old Testament characters gives a human touch to the divine truths contained in the Word of God. Esther is a book that reveals and demonstrates the sovereignty of God. Behind the scenes God is at work orchestrating circumstances and opportunities that have the potential to bring Him glory if we respond by faith and obedience.

I have written the study with five days of homework per week. For **the preschool mommies**, I have used a set of asterisks (**) to designate the questions that I want you to answer. If you find you have time to answer all questions, that is wonderful. However, if you are short on time, do the ones designated. For **the school-age moms and teen moms**, I trust you will be able to answer all the daily questions in your homework.

For **all** the age groups, at the end of each week I enclose a summary page. Devote some time to personal reflection on what you have learned through your week-long study of the Word of God. Write down your insights. Articulating the truths you have learned will help you assimilate them. The key to successfully incorporating the truths of the Scripture is to be about taking the *profound* truths of God's Word and making them *practical* in your life.

The goal of the Bible study is to learn how to appropriate the riches of our inheritance in Christ Jesus and live in power and victory. We have been made *heirs of God and fellow heirs with Christ* (Rom. 8:17). We are called to live up to the potential of our royal lineage. Too often we are content to snack and nibble on this world's offerings when we have been invited to sit and dine at the King's table! We are royal bluebloods. Peter writes, *But you are a chosen race, a royal priesthood, a holy nation, a people for God's own possession, that you may proclaim the excellencies of Him who has called you out of darkness into His marvelous light* (1 Pet. 2:9). Now is the time to learn how to *Live Like a Queen*.

Now get your Bible, a pen, and a teachable spirit. Let's get started. A wealth of truth awaits you. Prepare to be amazed!

Standing Near the Cross,

Jean Stockdale

Weekly Bible Studies

A Royal Relative

Read Assorted Passages

My nest is now empty. Craig and I reared and released two fine young men into the adult world. While the boys lived at home, I was the only female in a male-dominated household. I felt obligated to represent my gender well. Living with three men occasionally made that difficult! Actually I felt honored to be the only woman in a home marked by sports equipment, mud, sweat, and the aroma of aftershave. The noise level in a male-monopolized home often deafened. On the other hand I never had to get my own door, pump my own gas, or open a stubborn pickle jar. A man was always on call to help with those distasteful tasks. My family of men playfully called me "the queen." My husband actually treats me like a queen. He set a high standard of respect and honor for my boys to emulate. While my royal moniker is just an affectionate term of endearment, a shred of truth lies behind the title. At the moment of conversion I was placed into God's royal lineage.

**1. Read Romans 8:16-17. After your conversion experience what is your relationship to God?

_____

What is your relationship to Jesus Christ?

_____

Revelation 1:6 says, *And hath made us kings and priests unto God and his Father; to Him be glory and dominion for ever and ever. Amen* (KJV). Revelation 5:10 says, *And hast made us unto our God kings and priests; and we shall reign on the earth* (KJV). My betrothal to the King makes me a queen. Learning to live up to my potential as the Lord's royalty is my challenge.

We are about to begin a study about a young Jewish orphan who becomes queen of the Medo-Persian Empire by virtue of her marriage to King Ahasuerus. Our betrothal to the King of Glory instantly makes us members of the royal family, even as Esther's marriage to the king makes her the queen. Believe it or not, you and I are members of the heavenly monarchy! We are royal bluebloods. What a radical thought!

Colossians 1:13 says, *For He rescued us from the domain of darkness, and transferred us to the kingdom of His beloved Son, in whom we have redemption, the forgiveness of sins.* Paul said he had been sent to *proclaim the mystery of Christ* (Eph. 3:4) which is, *to be specific, that the Gentiles are fellow heirs and fellow members of the body, and fellow partakers of the promise in Christ Jesus through the gospel* (Eph. 3:6). We have become heirs of the *unfathomable riches of Christ* (Eph. 3:8). Like Esther, through your marriage covenant with Christ you are placed into the royal lineage.

Esther's marriage to the king elevates her to the royal position of queen. She has been a captive of the Persian Empire and has lived in poverty as one of the spoils of war. Her future is bleak. She is hopeless and helpless. Her destiny and her destination change the moment she marries the king. She instantly becomes a member of the royal family. She moves into the palace. She gets a new wardrobe complete with the crown jewels. Her diet changes. Her desires change. Her daily routine changes. Her status changes. She is swept into an opulent world that is totally different than the environment she has known—all because she marries the king of the Medo-Persian Empire. One moment a peasant; the next a queen!

Surely you already see the glaring similarities of Esther and a child of God. You are lost in your sin. You are held in bondage by sin, self, and Satan. But then you meet Jesus! At your conversion you are betrothed to King Jesus! Hallelujah! What a Savior! Deity invades your humanity. Your destiny and eternal destination dramatically change. The Holy Spirit of God moves into your human spirit. He radically and dramatically alters everything. Christ is your heavenly Bridegroom; you are His bride eagerly awaiting the Marriage Supper of the Lamb.

I am a creature of habit. Now, don't misunderstand me. I am not saying this necessarily is a good character quality; I merely state the facts. I am a creature of habit. I thrive on the monotonous repetition of a well-oiled routine. I am not particularly organized, but I do like the reassuring comfort of a daily routine. I find a sense of security in knowing what my day will hold and what is expected of me. Because God knows my particular bent, He constantly stirs my nest and interrupts my precious little routine! He does not want me to rely on my routine for security. He calls me to put my faith in Him and look to Jesus for my strength and support.

Having said that, I return to my original point. I am a creature of habit. Nearly every day I fix myself a turkey sandwich on wheat bread for lunch. I add lettuce, a pickle slice, and a dab of low-fat mayonnaise to round out my culinary creation. A handful of pretzels completes my gourmet feast. I usually head to the den, put my feet up, and catch the noon news while I munch my lunch. Several weeks ago I fixed my usual sandwich. Now remember, I *am* a creature of habit. I had started working on this Bible study; as I went through the motions of making my lunch, I was meditating on the study. With a pretzel stuffed in my mouth, I headed into the den to watch the local news. As I sat in my husband's leather chair and perched my feet up on the footstool, I picked up my sandwich and sank my teeth into my usual fare. To my surprise, I had omitted the meat! Even though I *am* a routine person, I was distracted by my study. I inadvertently omitted the turkey. This left me with a lettuce, pickle, and mayonnaise sandwich. Although all the ingredients were fresh and delicious, without the meat the sandwich was not particularly satisfying.

Similarly, as we begin this study, please understand that the same dilemma faces you. You can settle for being spoon-fed baby food at the children's table, or you can join the grown-ups and dine on filet mignon and Beef Wellington. Beloved, the choice is yours. Jesus Christ invites you to His table with an outrageous appetite for the things of God. Being declared a princess by your position in Christ is instantaneous; becoming a princess by practice is a process. Living like a queen involves more than just looking good in the crown! Will you accept His gracious invitation, or will you content yourself with the baby things of the gospel?

As for me, I have decided to feast on the meat of the Word. Choose for yourself!

2. Read Hebrews 5:12-14. What characterizes the Christian milk-drinkers?

_____

Who seeks solid food?

_____

What kind of appetite have you developed?

_____

Bible study without the meaty things of the Word of God never fully satisfies the deep longing of the heart. Beloved, I urge you to diligently pursue personal holiness and practical righteousness in your own life through the in-depth study of the Word of God. Just as my meatless meal was unsatisfying, so the Christian life will be tasteless and meaningless to you without the meat of God's Word active in your life.

**3. Peter gives us an analogy to which we, as moms, easily can relate. Read 1 Peter 2:1-3. What does Peter urge us to do?

_____

Why?

_____

Newborn babies are interested in only one thing. They do not care whether you have decorated the nursery with designer fabrics, an antique cradle, or your great-grandmother's rocking chair. They are unfazed by the expense you invested in making the baby's room a creative and colorful wonderland. They could care less if you hand-stenciled a wallpaper border or custom-ordered the blinds. Do they care if the diaper bag matches the car seat? Color-coordinating their wardrobe is immaterial to them. Newborns have one thing on their minds. They are single-mindedly determined to get food; if necessary they are willing to put up quite a fuss.

Beloved, develop a hunger for the Word of God. Refuse to be quieted until you find your satisfaction in Him! Join me as we study the Word of God together. Grab your Bible and a pen. Psalm 34:8 says, _O taste and see that the Lord is good._ Sample His delicacies. Develop an outrageous appetite for the Word of God. Pull up a chair; let's feast at His table!

A Good God

Read Assorted Passages

The Book of Esther is a dramatic presentation of the silent but sovereign ways of God. Unbeknownst to us He orchestrates the events and circumstances of our lives. While He waits in the wings for His cue to burst on the scene, God miraculously and mysteriously works in the lives of ordinary people to accomplish His extraordinary purpose and divine design. His unseen hand of providence guides us into the fulfillment of His perfect plan and the unspeakable joy of His perfect will. The invisible finger of God directs the mundane and minute details of our temporal existence to facilitate His eternal program.

Without mentioning the name of God, the Book of Esther clearly presents God's presence as His divine purpose is accomplished through human instruments. Nowhere else in Scripture is God's sovereign character displayed as it is in the Book of Esther yet without so much of a whisper of His name. In Esther's story His unspoken name only adds to the splendid spectacle of His majesty. Rather than painting a visual portrait of God the Father through the record of Esther, the writer reveals a watermark of the hand of God on the pages of history.

We often miss the silent working of God in our lives. This may be because of spiritual dullness on our part or a lack of spiritual sensitivity to the Lord. By His hidden hand of providence God directs the material universe in which we live.

**1. God controls the universe, even if from our limited, finite viewpoint it appears to be out of control. His creation, with the exception of humanity, obeys Him without question or hesitation. Read the account in Mark 4:35-41. (This is the same story Mt. 8:23-27 and Luke 8:22-52 record.) What do you learn about the Lord's sovereign control over His universe?

_____

God stands in the shadows of history and sovereignly and providentially orchestrates His divine purpose. God is at work. Sadly, people represent the only part of His creation that stubbornly resists and rebels against God's grace. Oh, that we would learn to walk in obedience and faith in God's divine revelation!

2. Look up Romans 11:33-34. What does this verse teach us about God's divine wisdom?

_____

God's wisdom is without equal. Human intellect and reasoning cannot comprehend His ways. Human logic cannot unravel the great mysteries of the finite mind of God or unlock His unfathomable sacred secrets.

3. Read Isaiah 55:8-9. What does this passage reveal about the infinite ways of God?

_____

God's Word is His divine revelation about Himself, His Son, and His glorious plan and purpose for our lives. As we immerse ourselves in the Word of God and saturate our soul with His truth, we begin to comprehend *with all the saints what is the breadth and length and height and depth* (Eph. 3:18) of our calling in Christ.

Studying the Book of Esther will cause us to become increasingly aware of God's providence and presence. Although the Book of Esther does not name His name, God is unmistakably and undeniably at work behind the scenes. Like the wind He silently but forcibly moves across the horizon of life. He influences and impacts the landscape without having form or figure. In John 3:8a Jesus says, *"The wind blows where it wishes and you hear the sound of it, but do not know where it comes from and where it is going."* Similarly, our Heavenly Father is involved in the circumstances of life. Like an animated composer directing a symphony orchestra, He stands on a celestial podium that is suspended in the heavenlies. His arms are raised. His baton is extended as He cues the strains of melodies that compose the songs of our lives. While we often are not aware of it, God orchestrates our circumstances. Providence is the means by which He directs everything—animate and inanimate, seen and unseen, good and evil—toward His perfect, final will. Ephesians 1:11 tells us that God *works all things after the counsel of His will*. Our God is in control of a world that seems upside down and inside out. Yet, our God reigns!

**4. Let's begin our study. Esther is first introduced to us in Esther 2:7. Based on your reading, write a description of Esther.

_____

_____

Esther, the heroine of our story, is an orphaned Jew who lives in exile in Persia. Her name means *star*. An unlikely hero, Esther is a vessel of God's own choosing *for such a time as this* (Esth. 4:14).

Four other main characters occupy the pages of the Book of Esther. Let me introduce them.

King Ahasuerus
This name is the Hebrew form of the Persian word. The Greeks changed that name to

Xerxes. Ahasuerus' reign lasted from 485-465 B.C. At the time Esther's story begins, Ahasuerus is in only the third year of his 21-year reign. During his reign Ahasuerus is considered to be the most powerful man on earth. He ruled over 127 provinces from India to Ethiopia. He is considered an erratic leader who rules by emotions and whims. The latter part of his reign is marked by alcoholism and bloodshed. Two of his officers ultimately assassinate him in his bedroom.

His Queen, Vashti

Queen Vashti's name means "beautiful woman". While the Scripture does not reveal a lot about Queen Vashti, we gather that she is a strong-willed woman. She stands up against her drunken husband's request to appear before his revelers. She knows her refusal will cost her the throne. She has every reason to assume her defiance will cost her life.

A Wicked Officer Named Haman

Haman is undeniably the villain of the story. He is a wealthy and influential officer in the king's court. His vehement hatred for God's chosen people leads to his death.

A Godly Jew Named Mordecai

Mordecai is a godly Jewish man living in Persia. At the death of her father and mother he takes Esther in and rears her as his own.

Just as Esther is divinely placed in the pages of history to fulfill God's purpose and plan, He providentially positions us for our good and His glory. As you study the life of Esther, you will begin to understand God's purpose for your life as a Christian woman, wife, and mom. You will learn to reign in this life. You will understand you have arrived at this time and place by God's doing, not by coincidence or chance. Our God is a good God!

An Ordinary Orphan

Read Assorted Passages

I had a sick headache. I quickly took some medications and stretched out across the foot of my bed. I sought the solace of sleep to ease the pain and render me temporally unaware of the throbbing in my temple. I was startled awake by the frantic voice of my dear friend, Renae Terrell. Renae currently works with me in my ministry, but at the time she was working for Craig in an office at the back of our property. Responding to the alarm in Renae's voice, I jumped up and made a futile effort to open my bleary eyes and clear my thick head. Groggy from the nap and the pain medication, I attempted to gather my befuddled thoughts and to focus on the crisis at hand. In a vain attempt to calm herself Renae squeaked out, "This is probably not as bad as it sounds, but the field next door is on fire. The fire is moving this way!" My sluggish brain refused to register what she had just said. My legs felt as if they had been immersed in a bucket of quick-dry cement. "What should we do?" she asked. "I have no idea," was my weak reply.

Let me step out of my story for one quick moment and tell you that I live on 10 acres in a very rural area in Fayette County. Although Craig and I love country living, we made a few concessions for the luxury of living outside the city limits. For instance, we live too far out to have a pizza delivered. We do not have garbage pickup or streetlights. We have septic tanks instead of sewers and a well instead of city water. We also are serviced by a volunteer fire department. Now, back to my story.

I did not know whom to call or what to do. Suddenly adrenaline took over. With Renae at my heel, I ran to the back of the property line. I was immediately seized with fear to see the wildfire consuming the brush and broom straw on the property behind us. I was enormously relieved to see that the volunteer fire department had already arrived. Firefighters heroically attempted to knock down the flames. They called in a bulldozer. The operator began to work in circles around the fire. It filled up a dirt border to contain the blaze.

My relief was short-lived as the fire moved in our direction. Fed by a gentle summer breeze, the blaze consumed our neighbor's barn and rapidly moved toward our property line!

Stunned into silence, Renae and I began to pray and ask for God's protection and wisdom. In God's goodness He put His hand of mercy and protection over our property, home, and office and quickly allowed the fire to be brought under control. How grateful we were to those faithful volunteers enlisted in the Fayette County volunteer fire department. God used them to spare our home and property.

Life so often seems like that wildfire, as it burns wildly out of control. Much of this life seems to be chaotic, random, and totally unmanageable. It seems to regularly threaten to catapult us headlong downhill at it somersaults and tumbles into disaster and destruction. Despite the uncertainty of life I know that my God is providentially in control of the universe in general and my life in particular. Daniel 4:35 says, *All the inhabitants of the earth are accounted as nothing, but He does according to His will in the host of heaven and among the inhabitants of earth.* In Psalm 118:23 the psalmist writes, *This is the Lord's doing; and it is marvelous in our eyes.* God knows what He is about in our lives; we can rest in His sovereign choices and His marvelous plans.

Perhaps no book in the Bible epitomizes this spiritual truth as does the story of Esther. Although this short book is without the mention of God, His quiet presence and immutable power cannot be denied. First Timothy 1:17 says, *Now to the King eternal, immortal, invisible, the only God, be honor and glory forever and ever. Amen.* What a lovely description of our God Who reigns among the hosts of heaven and rules in the lives of humanity. He is the unseen author and administrator of our lives.

Many years before Esther's story, a civil war divided the Jewish nation into two kingdoms. The northern kingdom was called Israel and was ruled by a series of wicked kings. The southern kingdom, Judah, fared a bit better. Some of her rulers were godly men, but the majority did not consistently walk with God.

God's judgment arrived for the northern kingdom in the form of captivity by the Assyrians. More than a hundred years later God used the Babylonians to attack Judah and carry the Jews of the southern kingdom into captivity. God would teach His people in affliction what they fail to learn in years of blessing and forbearance. About 100 years later Babylon was captured by the Medo-Persians. Around 485 B.C. Ahasuerus became king of the vast Persian Empire. The Book of Esther is set during the time when the Jews were living in exile in Persia.

When we are introduced to the heroine of our story, Esther is orphaned. Life has dealt Esther a terrible blow. We are not given details, but she suffers the loss of both her father and her mother. Without any siblings, Esther is left alone in her grief. Culturally widows and orphans have few options.

I pause for a moment and make this observation. Most women can easily identify with Esther's broken life. All of us have been hurt, disappointed, wounded, or crushed by life. For some the pain is a result of poor choices we made that continue to haunt us. We believe our checkered past has rendered us ineffective or possibly has disqualified us from serving God. Others suffer from pain inflicted by another. Physical or sexual abuse may have left you deeply scarred. Psychological abuse may be the culprit that left you with a warped sense of self-worth. Whatever the cause, most women can relate to Esther's brokenness. All of us bring some emotional baggage from our past into our adult lives. We step into the world of adulthood and suffer from the poor decisions we have made or the harm others have inflicted on us. Face it; to one degree or another we are all damaged goods.

Esther and her people are living in exile under the control of King Ahasuerus, a brutal and ruthless dictator. His closest adviser is a self-serving and wicked man named Haman. Haman despises the Jews and is bent on eliminating God's chosen people. Fortunately, God provides a way of escape. Esther, a young woman who is beautiful of form and face, will facilitate his plan. In His providence, God prepares a place for Esther in the home of her godly cousin, Mordecai, who *took her as his own daughter* (Esth. 2:7). Who better than Esther can teach us that God can take all the broken pieces of our lives and fashion them into a magnificent mosaic for His own glory?

**1. Have you ever felt insignificant or even invisible?

_____

Have you ever wondered what God's purpose and plan is for your life?

_____

Well, I have good news for you! Read Psalm 139:13-16. What do we learn about our divine design?

_____

What does that teach us about our worth?

_____

Let me share a word of personal testimony. When I was 24 years old, I was introduced to the Lord under the preaching ministry of Dr. Adrian Rogers. Before that time I had very little exposure to the Word of God. Consequently, I had some serious issues, not the least of which was a poor self-image. For 24 years my unsaved condition had led me to make many bad decisions. I brought substantial guilt into my Christian experience. As a new believer I felt like a miserable failure. I knew I would go to heaven when I died, but I doubted my ability to properly live the Christian life. Enamored by the Scriptures and deeply in love with Jesus, I began to read and study the Word of God, but I was quite certain I could never make any permanent changes in my life. I was sure I was destined for defeat and headed for heartache.

As I began to study the Scriptures I found myself face-to-face with a reality I could not fully comprehend but could not deny: Jesus knew me completely and yet, He still loved me unconditionally. Romans 5:8 says, *But God demonstrates His own love toward us, in that while we were yet sinners, Christ died for us.* This truth was too magnificent to comprehend. God loved me unconditionally! He showed His love for me by sending His own dear Son to die in my place. Unspeakable love! First John 3:1 says, *See how great a love the Father has bestowed on us, that we would be called children of God; and such we are.* Unfathomable truth! While I could not grasp this kind of love with my limited understanding, I did begin to receive it by faith and walk in the glorious truth that God loves me. Despite my flaws, failures, and frailties, God loves me! The final piece of truth and understanding happened when I read Ephesians 1:4. It says, *He chose us in Him before the foundation of the world, that we would be holy and blameless before Him.* Before God created this vast universe—before life began—I was on God's heart. He knew me! I cannot tell you how liberating this truth was to me. God loved me regardless of my performance. Hallelujah! What a Savior! As the reality of these truths penetrated my thoughts, renewed my mind, and reprogrammed my thinking, I began to walk in the authenticity of God's divine revelation. I began to reign in this life.

Esther surely struggles with her self-concept and worth. The death of her parents plunges this young woman into unimaginable depths of heart-wrenching agony. She surely believes that her life is without meaning or purpose. She has no means of support. As she surveys her lot in life, she feels helpless and hopeless. Little does she know God is silently and invisibly working behind the scenes of history. In God's divine plan Esther will become His vessel of honor. She will rescue her people. Who but God can do such things?

Esther is an ordinary orphan, but God has a plan. Just as God has a purpose for Esther, He has a perfect will for your life as well. The essence of the Christian life is discovering daily what God ordains and following after Him with a surrendered heart. *"For I know the plans that I have for you," declares the Lord, "plans for welfare and not for calamity to give you a future and a hope"* (Jer. 29:11). Together, as we study the life of Esther, I pray you will discover God's perfect plan and purpose for your life.

A Drunken Disaster

Read Esther 1:1-22

The Book of Esther begins with a party being held in the palace with King Ahasuerus acting as host. On the surface this tidbit of information does not seem unusual. Royals often hold banquets. The scope of this party is what sets it apart. This extravaganza lasts 180 days. An estimated 15,000 people attend. For six months the king plies his guests with gourmet goodies and tantalizing treats. In the great hall of the palace decadence and delicacies mingle. They dull the minds and sear the consciences of his guests.

This pagan celebration has all the usual components. The music is loud, the dancing is raunchy, and the wine flows like water. Groaning banquet tables boast of sumptuous dishes. A well-trained staff attends to the whims of the partygoers. Plates are passed; glasses are filled. Lavish displays of King Ahasuerus' fortunes are flaunted. Parades are organized to show off the king's legions of slaves and spoils of his conquests. For six months the king flaunts *the riches of his royal glory and the splendor of his great majesty* (Esth. 1:4).

The party is most likely a planning session for the impending war with Greece. The king not only wants to discuss upcoming military strategies, he also wants to impress the leaders of his provinces with his incredible wealth and his irrefutable power. The king is defined by his achievements and accumulation of wealth; he puts them all on display. At the end of his six-month marathon banquet the king throws a seven-day drinking party.

**1. Read Esther 1:5-8. Describe the party and the palace setting.

_____

_____

The king invites everybody, from the greatest to the least. The king attempts to impress his subjects with the splendor of his possessions and the status of his power. His people arrive by the thousands to experience the banquet and the revelry. *Drinks were served in golden vessels of various kinds, and the royal wine was plentiful according to the king's bounty* (Esth. 1:7). His guests are free to drink or decline. With the king footing the bill many drink heavily.

King Ahasuerus attempts to garner praise and adoration by displaying his trophies and trinkets of wealth. Wine flows like water. It blurs the minds of his guests ; it warps their judgment and dulls their senses. In Proverbs 31:3-5 King Lemuel records the words his mother taught him. *Do not give your strength to women, or your ways to that which destroys kings. It is not for kings, O Lemuel, it is not for kings to drink wine, or for rulers to desire strong drink, for they will drink and forget what is decreed, and pervert the rights of all the afflicted.* Sadly, King Ahasuerus' mother has not taught him the truth of God's Word.

Although the Book of Esther takes place many centuries ago, the issues addressed in it are as current as today's news. The people of Persia, as well as many of its leaders, are enamored with the empty pursuits of the world. The glamorous, opulent world into which Esther is swept sadly mirrors our decadent world today. Like Esther's world, our modern society is obsessed with any behavior that appeals to the basest desires of depraved humanity.

As in Esther's day, a believer easily can be contaminated by the pollution of the world's philosophies. To combat the world's corruption we daily renew our minds with the Word of God and surrender to the indwelling Holy Spirit. In John 15:19 Jesus says, *"If you were of the world, the world would love its own; but because you are not of the world, but I chose you out of the world, because of this the world hates you."* Jesus prays to the Father, *"I do not ask You to take them out of the world, but to keep them from the evil one"* (John 17:15). While we live in this world, we are not to be of this world.

**2. Name some ways the world attempts to conform us to its way of thinking and acting.

_____

Read James 4:1-5. What does this passage teach us about friendship with the world?

_____

What is the end result when we let down our guard and embrace the world's ways?

_____

How can we avoid the snare of the world's deception and decadence?

_____

Guard your hearts and minds, lest you fall victim of the temptations of the world, the flesh, and the devil. The world's viewpoint is quietly and insidiously being spread. Learn to walk circumspectly to avoid its corruption.

The only way to combat the enemy's lies is to recognize them and counteract them with the truth. God's Word is our plumb line. Knowing His truth will ensure our victory.

**3. Read Romans 12:2. According to this verse what is the secret to success in the Christian life if we are to avoid the pitfalls of the world?

_____

The secret to remaining steadfast in the midst of a shifting world is to be anchored to the Lord Jesus Christ and His Word. As the strong tides of change threaten to undercut our moorings, we hold on to Jesus, the *anchor of the soul* (Heb. 6:19).

In another area of the palace Queen Vashti gives a banquet for the women. King Ahasuerus and his guests are becoming increasingly drunk with wine. Loud music. Wild dancing. Gluttonous indulging. Gorging on delicious delicacies and rich pastries. Drinking in excess. The mens' bachelor party is reaching a drunken crescendo. The stage is set for a royal request, a regal refusal, a terrible tantrum, and a mad monarch!

A Royal Ruckus

Read Esther 1:1-22

As the Book of Esther opens, we are introduced to King Ahasuerus, who is in the midst of hosting a six-month-long party. The extravaganza is capped off with a week-long event. After seven days of drinking and revelry the crowd has become sufficiently drunk with wine and gorged with the bounty of the palace's banqueting tables. Plentiful alcohol leads to excessive drinking, debauchery, and disgraceful behavior. With their minds numbed from the effects of alcohol and their bodies sluggish from the steady glut of epicurean delicacies, the guests grow restless and look for new ways to satisfy their unrestrained lusts. All the stops have been pulled out for this bash, which is rapidly deteriorating into nothing more than a drunken orgy.

For months the king displays all his magnificent finery and accumulated wealth. The king, now quite drunk, realizes that he has one more treasure—Queen Vashti—that has not been prominently displayed! With drunken breath and slurred speech the king directs his servants to send word to the queen to join them.

**1. Read Esther 1:10-11. What does King Ahasuerus command his eunuchs to do?

_____

Bible scholars are not absolutely certain of the true meaning of the king's command. Some believe the king simply asks for the queen to parade unveiled before the men of Susa so they might admire her beauty. That request alone would have been scandalous in a Persian court. Especially in the presence of men, Oriental women were generally extremely modest and covered themselves discreetly. The queen may believe this violates her dignity. After all, she is not one of the king's trophies to be put on public display.

Some Bible commentators think the queen refuses because she is pregnant; a public appearance would be unthinkable. If this is the case, her refusal is understandable. However, most commentators believe that King Ahasuerus actually commands his queen to parade naked before this drunken crowd of revelers and to wear only her crown. While we cannot emphatically know the king's intent, we know his request is unconscionable!

**2. Read Esther 1:12. What is Queen Vashti's response to the king's cruel command?

Queen Vashti's refusal to be publicly humiliated and debased before the lustful gazes of hundreds of drunken men sends shock waves throughout the king's court. Who would dare defy a direct order of the king? A royal ruckus ensues.

I admire the queen's indignation at the king's shameful request. The queen refuses to give the drunken crowds the opportunity to leer at her and satisfy their depraved desires. The result would amount to little more than royal pornography. The king, whose mental capacity and judgment obviously is diminished by his inebriated state, is intent on using his wife to provoke others to jealousy. What he asks is not submission but sexual slavery. Marriage, even in royal cases, does not give a husband license to fulfill his basest fantasies by using his wife as a sexual object. Although Queen Vashti is right to refuse the insulting request of her husband, King Ahasuerus is furious with his wife's defiance. He is the most powerful leader in the Medo-Persian Empire and is not accustomed to having his royal requests refused.

Because the biblical principle of submission often is misunderstood and maligned, we are wise to pause in our study of Esther and pursue God's divine perspective on this difficult subject.

A perpetual struggle between men and women is a direct result and bitter consequence of Adam and Eve's sin (see Gen. 3:16). Since the fall, wives naturally have an innate desire to usurp their husband's headship. Husbands typically respond by trying to impose a despotic, authoritarian rule over their wives. This continual wrestling for headship endangers many marriages today and threatens to push them to the brink of disaster.

The key to every successful Christian marriage is submission. Because submission runs contrary to our human nature, the filling of the Holy Spirit is required to rise above the downward pull of the flesh.

In Christ men and women are spiritual equals. In the Lord *there is neither male nor female; for you are all one in Christ Jesus* (Gal. 3:28). In marriage we become heirs together *of the grace of life* (1 Pet. 3:7). However, God assigns roles to husbands and wives to benefit the family unit. God calls the husband to be the servant leader of the home. God gives wives the role of submission to his leadership.

In a similar way, parents are given authority in the family; children are told to follow. Colossians 3:20 says, *Children, be obedient to your parents in all things, for this is well-pleasing to the Lord.*

Ephesians 5:22 says, *Wives, be subject to your own husbands, as to the Lord.* Taken out of context, this verse has caused many husbands to repress their wives and many wives to be resentful and rebellious. Standing alone this verse seems unfair and arbitrary. When studying the Word, avoid taking verses out of context. The context of this verse includes the Holy

Spirit's instruction for mutual submission among believers. Ephesians 5:21 says, *Be subject to one another in the fear of Christ.* Such holy living emanates from the Holy Spirit's infilling and power.

God has ordained a hierarchal structure throughout the universe and particularly in the home. First Corinthians 11:3 says, *The head of every man is Christ; and the head of the woman is the man; and the head of Christ is God* (KJV). God creates Adam first and gives him the position of headship. Then He creates Eve and denotes a subordinate but not a subservient position in relation to Adam. God's plan requires the husband to be under the authority of God and over the wife as a loving servant leader.

Jesus willingly submits to the Father even though He is co-equal and co-eternal with Him. In John 12:49 Jesus says, "*For I did not speak on My own initiative, but the Father Himself who sent Me has given Me a commandment as to what to say, and what to speak*" Jesus existed *in the form of God,* yet He *emptied Himself, taking the form of a bond-servant* and became *obedient to the point of death, even death on a cross* (see Phil. 2:5-11). Submission has nothing to do with value or worth and everything to do with order and authority.

While submission is required of a godly wife, sacrifice is commanded of a godly husband. As the spiritual leader of the home, a godly man is *to love (his wife), just as Christ also loved the church and gave Himself up for her* (Eph. 5:25). No woman has ever had any problem submitting to a man who loves her as Christ loves His bride, the church. A godly man consults with his wife, delegates certain tasks to her, and carefully considers her insights and instincts, but he is responsible for making final decisions. He will give an account to God for his oversight of his family.

The husband's authority has a limitation. If he requests something contrary to God's revealed Word, the wife is not obligated. At this point he has overstepped the limits of his authority. Colossians 3:18 says, *Wives, be subject to your own husbands, as is fitting in the Lord.* If at any point the husband violates his God-given authority by making a request that violates God's Word, the wife is not compelled to oblige.

The same principle applies to all forms of authority. Acts 5:29 says, *We ought to obey God rather than men.* If the request violates Scripture, this principle supersedes the passages on submission. Queen Vashti courageously refuses her husband's demeaning request. Her bravery costs her the throne but leaves her dignity intact!

What about a husband that is immature in the Lord or an unbeliever? Is a Christian wife still obligated to submit to an unsaved or spiritually immature husband? Unless he commands his wife to disobey God, a godly wife is to submit herself to her husband. In doing so, he may be won to Christ *without a word* as he observes the chaste conduct and *imperishable quality of a gentle and quiet spirit* formed in his wife by her obedience to the Holy Spirit of God (1 Pet. 3:1-5).

The model for a Christian home is the Lord Jesus Christ, who has lifted the concept of marriage to a higher plane than ever could have been conceived outside a personal relationship with Him. Marriage is God's plan in the Garden of Eden to make paradise complete. By instituting marriage, God has a visual aid to demonstrate the reality of Christ and His church.

Sin spoils God's picture designed to be an earthly display of a heavenly ideal. Sin is humanity's ruin; Christ is God's remedy. While sin and self continue to plague the Christian home, the home remains an outpost of heaven in the midst of a sin-cursed world. Home is a safe place in which family and friends can experience the wonders of God's mysterious purposes and plans.

Husbands are to lead their families with loving servant leadership. Wives are to submit to their own husbands. Children are to obey their parents. This is God's divine blueprint for families. To ignore or violate His holy plan for the family is to invite disaster and to incur hurt and heartache. Surrender to God's heavenly purpose for your life and your home.

Weekly Summary

Please record insights gleaned from this week's study.

A Raging Ruler

Read Esther 1:1-22

Secular history records the well-known temper of King Ahasuerus. So great are his well-documented fits of anger that some have suggested that he suffers from some sort of abnormality. Whether the king is a certifiable rageaholic or merely given to fits of temper, we cannot be certain. We do know that Queen Vashti's refusal to be publicly humiliated and debased greatly displeases him and sends him into a fit of seething fury. Obviously, the volume of alcohol that the king has consumed contributes to his unrestrained anger.

Esther 1:12b says, *Then the king became very angry and his wrath burned within him.* King Ahasuerus is furious with the queen for refusing his order. She publicly humiliates him in front of his subjects and undermines his power and authority. After weeks of overindulgence, his drunken state dulls his mind and clouds his judgment. His wrath knows no bounds. In his mind Queen Vashti's refusal to obey a royal command is tantamount to treason.

King Ahasuerus is in a quandary. He is angry and embarrassed. He can not overlook the queen's public defiance. The king takes counsel with his wise men, *who understood the times.* These are advisers who *had access to the king's presence and sit in the first place in the kingdom.* Interestingly these seven men have instant access to the king. Without risking death the queen can not appear before him unless he summons her.

The king, surrounded by his court counselors, considers his next course of action. Don't miss this irony! A drunken king seeks the advice of his equally inebriated counselors about his marital problems. Nothing about this scenario bodes well.

Like the king, in an emergency we often are tempted to seek ill-advised counsel. Turning to worldly advisors in time of crisis is unwise at best and dangerous at worst. Because we often have not invested the time and energy to renew our minds with the Word of God, we can be unwittingly influenced by the world's philosophies and counsel.

**1. Read Psalm 1:1-6. What insight can you glean from this passage?

How foolish to attempt to mix the wisdom of the world with the mind of Christ and expect an outcome that honors the Lord!

2. Read Proverbs 1:5. What does this verse teach about wise counsel?

_____

Seeking guidance is prudent, but consult a Bible-believing counselor. Proverbs 12:15 says, *The way of a fool is right in his own eyes, but a wise man is he who listens to counsel.* Also, continually saturate your soul with the Word of God. Aggressively pursue a life marked by personal holiness and practical righteousness.

The king looks to Memucan, his lead counsel, and asks, "*According to the law, what is to be done with Queen Vashti, because she did not obey the command of King Ahasuerus delivered by the eunuchs?*" What begins as a conflict between a husband and wife is quickly escalating into a crisis of national proportions.

**3. Read Esther 1:16-19. The king consults with his wise men. What conclusion has Memucan reached about the queen's response to the king's request?

_____

What is Memucan's concern?

_____

What does he suggest?

_____

We assume Vashti has great sway over the women of the empire. The king and his court agree that her disobedience will give wives courage to respond similarly to their mates. Memucan said, "*This day the ladies of Persia and Media who have heard of the queen's conduct will speak in the same way to all the king's princes, and there will be plenty of contempt and anger*" (Esth. 1:18). Strengthened by the queen's disobedience, women throughout the kingdom might go on strike and abandon their wifely duties. Thus they will display *contempt and anger*. The only course of action is to depose the queen as a result of her impudence. Such harsh consequences will insure the obedience of wives everywhere.

Memucan's overreaction to the queen's refusal seems to indicate problems in his own household. I cannot help but think Memucan has issues at home and seizes on a chance to address his marital problems by legislating obedience from the wives! His counsel may have been a thinly veiled attempt to keep his own wife in her place. The other counselors heartily agree with Memucan. If the king cannot make an example of Vashti, all the men can lose total control of their wives! This threatens the fragile ego of these self-made men and endangers their tyrannical rule of their own households.

The king is advised to respond decisively to the queen's audacity to avoid a national uprising. Memucan said, "*If it pleases the king, let a royal edict be issued by him and let it be written in the laws of the Persia and Media so that it cannot be repealed, that Vashti may no longer come into the presence of King Ahasuerus, and let the king give her royal position to another who is more worthy than she"* (Esth. 1:19). Such a proclamation will certainly strike fear in the heart of any wife who considers resisting her husband's demands.

A royal edict is issued and written in the laws of the Persia and Media. According to a fundamental law of the Medo-Persian Empire a decree, once entered, cannot be altered—even by the king.

Queen Vashti is deposed from being queen and banished from the king's presence for life. The Bible is not clear what becomes of the queen. While some believe the queen is executed, most Bible commentators believe she is vanquished to an outlying area of the palace. Vashti loses her crown but keeps her dignity intact.

As a backdrop for a story that demonstrates the silent presence of a sovereign God, the author of Esther spotlights the conflict between Vashti and the king. Into this scene God divinely places our heroine, Esther.

A Legalistic Leader

Read Esther 1:1-22

The king is infuriated by Queen Vashti's refusal to obey him. He is not used to being defied. His public humiliation combined with his drunken state makes him bristle with rage. I, for one, applaud the queen's decision to refuse to condescend to the demeaning command of the king. The queen's beauty is meant for her husband alone and is not to be put on public display to satisfy the perverse lusts of a drunken crowd.

King Ahasuerus' response to the queen's rejection is to attempt to legislate obedience. Esther 1:20 says, *And when the king's edict which he will make is heard throughout all his kingdom, great as it is, then all women will give honor to their husbands, great and small.* The king foolishly believes he can legislate love, command compliance, and order obedience. The king *sent letters to all the king's provinces, to each province according to its script and to every people according to their language, that every man should be the master in his own house* (Esth. 1:22). Obedience and submission, which spring forth out of a heart of love, cannot be legislated. The king thinks he can solve a problem with an ironclad edict written into the Law of the Medes and the Persians. Compliance cannot be coerced.

This attitude is at the heart of legalism. Legalism is the attempt to externally control behavior with strict adherence to rules and regulations. It can be manifested by an unbeliever or a believer. An unbeliever can mimic the Christian life (for a season) by engaging in religious ritual. Ultimately his/her legalistic imitation will be revealed. John writes, *They went out from us, but they were not really of us; for if they had been of us, they would have remained with us; but they went out, so that it would be shown that they all are not of us* (1 John 2:19).

People historically seek to save themselves through the accumulation of good works and self-righteousness. They rely on human effort rather than humbly casting themselves on the grace and mercy of God through Christ. Nothing is quite as unappealing or unsatisfying as is religion without Christ.

No amount of good works or religious activity can gain us entrance into heaven. Salvation is through the Lord Jesus Christ. Second Timothy 1:8-9 says, *Therefore do not be ashamed of the testimony of our Lord, or of me His prisoner, but join with me in suffering for the gospel according to the power of God, who has saved us, and called us with a holy calling, not according to our works, but according to His own purpose and grace which was granted us in Christ Jesus from all eternity.* The person who solemnly believes he or she can work his/her way into heaven does not understand the depravity of man nor the holiness of God.

Salvation is by grace through faith in Jesus Christ. Acts 16:31 says, *Believe in the Lord Jesus, and you will be saved.* Acts 4:12 says, *And there is salvation in no one else; for there is no other name under heaven that has been given among men, by which we must be saved.*

**1. Look up Ephesians 2:8-9. God has one way for salvation. What is it?

_____

_____

Salvation is by grace through faith in Jesus Christ; not a result of good works. Salvation is a gift extended by a holy God to sinful humanity by the shed blood of Jesus Christ. Jesus is the once-for-all-time sacrificial substitute. He is *the Lamb of God who takes away the sin of the world* (John 1:29). While He died for the sin of the world, His blood is applied only to the account of those who receive Him by grace through faith.

**2. Read Titus 3:3-7. What was your condition before your conversion?

_____

What does this passage teach about your glorious salvation in Jesus Christ?

_____

Although many Christians recognize that salvation is by grace through faith, they attempt to live the Christian life by legalistically adhering to a list of rules and regulations. Legalism steals the joy, sours the soul, and stifles the spirit. Legalism is a vain attempt to use willpower to control the flesh and force the outward behavior to conform to rules people make. This method of managing the flesh with the flesh short-circuits the power of the indwelling Holy Spirit. It produces the temporary appearance of godliness. This method merely strengthens the indwelling flesh rather than crucifying it through obedience to Christ. Putting the flesh to death is necessary. It cannot be reformed. It cannot be constrained by external compliance to religious rituals. The flesh requires a death blow by the Spirit of God. To live the victorious Christian life repeating this daily will be necessary. This faith-based life desperately relies on Christ in us, the hope of glory. Faith is accessed by obedience to the Word of God, dependence on the Spirit of God, and confidence in the Son of God.

Through faith in Christ we have been *set free from the law of sin and of death* (Rom. 8:2) and raised to *walk in newness of life* (Rom. 6:4). Colossians 3:1-3 says, *If then you have been raised up with Christ, keep seeking the things above, where Christ is, seated at the right hand of God. Set your mind on the things above, and not on the things that are on earth. For you have died and your life is hidden with Christ in God.* In Christ we have been set free.

In Christ we have the power to crucify the flesh. We dare not corrupt grace with legalism. Learn to walk in the liberty that Christ has provided. Refuse to be placed under the bondage of legalism.

3. Read Galatians 5:1. In this verse, about what does Paul warn us?

_____

Christians who do not understand the liberty of Christ want to place us under the bondage of legalism—*a yoke of slavery*. Do not allow yourselves to be held captive by religious rules and rituals of self-made religion.

We also have another threat to our freedom in Christ—a threat that is just as dangerous as legalism is to our spiritual well-being.

**4. Read Galatians 5:13. What is Paul's concern?

_____

Liberty, when abused, results in licentiousness. Our freedom in Christ does not give us license to sin carelessly under the auspiciousness of grace. Paul is horrified by this thought. In Romans 6:1-2 he writes, *What shall we say then? Are we to continue in sin so that grace may increase? May it never be! How shall we who died to sin still live in it?* License and legalism are ditches on both sides of a narrow path called *liberty*. In 1 Corinthians 6:12 Paul writes, *All things are lawful for me, but not all things are profitable.* Legalism attempts to live the Christian life by strict adherence to a list of rules. License allows for indiscriminate sinning under the guise of grace. Either trap is lethal to the victorious Christian life.

As we obey God's Word, we experience liberty. Our obedience to Christ springs forth from a yielded heart and a surrendered soul. We serve Him gladly from *devotion* rather than from *duty*. Our willing submission is out of the overflow of our devotional life and love for the Lord Jesus Christ. Our devotion cannot be mandated by legalism or the laws of the Medes and the Persians, for that matter. Our love is not distorted by license. It flows freely from hearts that are wholly His.

King Ahasuerus attempted to demand obedience and legislate love. This simply cannot be done. Tyranny breeds rebellion.

A Proper Perspective

Read Esther 1:1-22

King Ahasuerus and his queen obviously have some marital issues. Marriages among royalty were often arranged for political gain and were devoid of love. This may be their situation. Without further revelation we can only surmise the state of their mutual affection. However, we can deduce that the royal husband and wife were unbelievers. Obviously we would not expect to gain insight into God's holy matrimony by observing the union of those outside a personal relationship with Him. The Word of God is our only source of truth.

The Bible is not only profound, God's Word is practical. Applying the truths found in the Word requires the enlightenment of the Holy Spirit of God. Paul writes, *But a natural man does not accept the things of the Spirit of God, for they are foolishness to him; and he cannot understand them, because they are spiritually appraised* (1 Cor. 2:14). When we approach the Word of God with a surrendered soul and an obedient heart, God will speak through His written revelation.

God ordained the institution of marriage in the Garden of Eden before the fall. Even in a perfect environment He knew Adam needed a suitable helpmeet. Enter Eve. God's design for marriage has a much greater purpose than companionship or procreation.

**1. As incredible as it may seem, God wants to use the marriage relationship to illustrate the relationship between Christ and His bride, the church. Read Ephesians 5:22-33. Paul details the characteristics of a godly marriage relationship. What role is assigned to the husband?

_____

What role is assigned to the wife?

_____

What does the Christian marriage picture?

_____

Marriage is to represent the love relationship between Christ and His bride, the church. The Christian home is to be God's visual aid in the midst of a sin-sick world to demonstrate God's plan and purpose for the family. Philippians 2:15-16 says, *Prove yourselves to be blameless and innocent, children of God above reproach in the midst of a crooked and perverse generation, among whom you appear as lights in the world, holding fast the word of life.* While original sin has marred the image, God intends for the Christian home to demonstrate the saving knowledge of Jesus Christ.

**2. Read 1 Peter 3:7-9. Describe a godly husband's attitude toward his wife?

_____

According to this passage, how will a Christian husband and wife respond to each other?

_____

Christian couples that fully realize their perspective roles in the marriage relationship are not in competition with one another. The husband will be a servant leader in the home; he will not assume the role of a dictator. A godly wife will be a suitable helpmeet to her husband and not strive to usurp her husband's authority. Both will be invested in living in harmony and helping his or her mate reach his or her full potential in Christ.

Sadly, King Ahasuerus has no concept of God's plan for his life, his reign, or his marriage. As believers in Christ we have God's written Word and His indwelling Holy Spirit which enables us to live and walk in victory.

God's Spirit is our internal control. In John 14:18 Jesus says, "*I will not leave you as orphans, I will come to you.*" In John 14:26 Jesus says, "*But the Helper, the Holy Spirit, whom the Father will send in My name, He will teach you all things, and bring to your remembrance all that I said to you.*"

God's Word is our external control. In 2 Timothy 3:16 Paul writes, *All Scripture is inspired by God and profitable for teaching, for reproof, for correction, for training in righteousness; so that the man of God may be adequate, equipped for every good work.* Hebrews 4:12 says, *For the word of God is living and active and sharper than any two-edged sword, and piercing as far as the division of soul and spirit, of both joints and marrow, and able to judge the thoughts and intentions of the heart.* Beloved, we are to submit to the Spirit of God and obey the Word of God. We are to walk in the truth for His honor and glory.

A Bashful Beauty

Read Esther 1:1-23

Four years pass. In the intervening years King Ahasuerus (also known as Xerxes) has been off fighting a disastrous war with Greece. His ignominious defeat depletes the coffers of the Persian empires and discredits him in the eyes of his subjects. He returns to the palace a broken man. Historians tell us he self-medicates with overindulgences of every kind. He has affairs with the wives of his military officers; this further damages his reputation and reduces his support.

Esther 2:1 says, *After these things when the anger of King Ahasuerus had subsided, he remembered Vashti and what she had done and what had been decreed against her.* The passing of time smooths off the rough edges of the queen's offense. Now he only remembers her beauty, her warmth, and her kindness. The king's anger long since has subsided; he longs for another to replace his deposed queen.

The king's attendant suggests a plan. The kingdom will be canvassed for beautiful young women. Officers of the king will traverse the land and bring them to the palace in Susa. There they will be placed in the harem. Hegai, the king's eunuch, will oversee them. He will train them in royal protocol and supply them with cosmetics and beauty aids. *"Then let the young lady who pleases the king be queen in place of Vashti." And the matter pleased the king, and he did accordingly* (Esth. 2:4). To our modern way of thinking this manner of gathering candidates to replace the queen seems outrageous. Even by Persian standards, it is a bit unusual. Most queens are chosen from prominent royal families.

Besides having one or more wives, Persian kings typically had concubines. These were women who arrived as virgins to the king's bed and then lived in luxurious accommodations in his harem. Such practices were quite common. They serve to depict how power was used and abused in the Persian court. Everyone was at the disposal of the king's personal whim.

King Ahasuerus does not seem to be looking for a one-night encounter. He has a large harem full of women. Also, he can have any woman in the kingdom he wants. He does not want a sexual encounter; he wants a wife. He is lonely for companionship with a woman who cares for him.

In this chapter we are introduced to Mordecai and Esther. Mordecai is a Jew of the tribe of Benjamin; he lives in exile in Susa. Since the Jews have been in captivity for 120 years, we assume Mordecai is not born until after Jerusalem falls. His ancestors are taken captive from Jerusalem; he is born as their offspring in captivity. Mordecai is at the citadel in Susa, but his responsibilities are not made clear.

In this chapter we also meet Esther for the first time. Esther is a young Jewish orphan living in exile. Were it not for the kindness of her cousin, Mordecai, she is destined to a life of destitution and deprivation. He takes her in and treats her *as his own daughter* (Esth 2:7).

Esther's Jewish name is *Hadassah*, which means "a fragrant shrub." Even in an ungodly place her life proves to be a fragrance of the presence of God. For Hebrew people to have both a Hebrew name and a name taken from the culture in which they live is not uncommon. This indicates Esther's duo-citizenship. Jewish by birth, she is forced to live in exile in Persia.

Esther has no idea of what has transpired in the royal palace. She is unaware of the turbulent storm resulting from Queen Vashti's refusal to obey the king's lewd command. She does not know she is standing on the threshold of a divine appointment that will dramatically change her life and ultimately alter the course of Jewish history. As she awakens that fateful morning, she thinks her day will be like any other in her rather ordinary existence.

As Esther goes about her menial tasks, she has no idea of the possibilities that will soon open up to her under the providential hand of God. God is silently working behind the scenes of history's stage. He is continually moving. He is rearranging events and changing minds until He brings about opportunities that will set His perfect plan into motion. God works in carnal and secular settings. Difficult circumstances, stubborn hearts, or persistent rebellion will not thwart His purposes or plans. God is not frozen with fear or paralyzed with panic. Even when our lives appear to be frantically racing out of control, God is quietly and sovereignly in charge. Psalm 27:1 says, *The Lord is my light and my salvation; whom shall I fear? The Lord is the defense of my life; whom shall I dread?* Learn to trust Him. Learn to rest in Him.

The monotony of life often serves to dull our sensitivity to God. First Corinthians 2:9 says, *Things which eye has not seen and ear has not heard and which have not entered the heart of man, all that God has prepared for those who love Him.* Learn to live in holy expectation. At any moment your great God might be about to break into your life and dramatically change its course.

As we approached our boys' teen-age years, I dreaded the day when they would learn to drive. I was so frightened by the prospect of my boys being behind the wheel of a vehicle. Should a child who cannot remember his lunch money be given the opportunity to operate a motor vehicle? Frankly, 16 seems too young to be given the opportunity or the responsibility of driving a car. For those of you who are currently in the carpool season of life and you feel that you live in your minivan carting children from one activity to another, may I remind you of something worse? One day your child is going to get his/her license and drive your car! A teen behind the wheel is a mother's greatest fear! As I wrestled with this fear God reminded of Psalm 127:1 which says, *Unless the Lord builds the house, they labor in vain who build it; unless the Lord guards the city, the watchman* (that was me!) *keeps awake in vain.* I knew the time had arrived to cast this burden on the Lord and to rest in His providential care of my family.

**1. Read Psalm 121:1-8. Meditate on these glorious truths. What can you learn about God's care of His children?

How can you relate this truth to your mothering?

Mothering is tough work. Learn to work in partnership with God to build eternal things into your child's life. Learn to trust Him to do what only He can do. In Philippians 2:13 Paul writes, *For it is God who is at work in you, both to will and to work for His good pleasure.* When you learn to rest in Him, you discover that He is working in you to give you the desire and the power to accomplish His will! What a glorious truth!

God moves on His own schedule and is not constrained by the measure of time like we are. Therefore, we often wrongly conclude that God is not at work in our situation. We often fear God has forgotten us or somehow is unaware of our situation. Because we do not see Him working, we deduce that He is not. This is the wonder of God's sovereign ways. God is always at work behind the scenes, although His presence often is obscured by the repetitiveness of our ordinary lives.

Actually any life that has been touched by the hand of God can never be ordinary again! I know of nothing more exciting than being a Christian. As believers we are sharing the life of Jesus Christ. We have become a part of the relentless, invincible purpose of almighty God. The Christian life pulsates with divine energy and cannot be explained apart from God. What could be more exciting?!

The Jews, living in exile in Persia, surely believe God had abandoned them. Nothing can be further from the truth. God's heart remains attached to His chosen people. To keep His covenant promise of preservation, God is obligated to protect them even on foreign soil. He will use Esther, an unknown orphan, as a vital part of His plan to protect the Jews from extermination. Events have been set in motion that will sweep her into the center of God's providential plan for His people. Apart from her knowledge, a vacancy has been opened up in the royal palace. God is waiting in the wings to introduce His newest star!

A Gorgeous Girl

Read Esther 1:1-23

Esther is *beautiful of form and face* (Esth. 2:7). Her natural beauty catches the eye of the king's servants. Esther 2:8 says, *So it came about when the command and decree of the king were heard and many young ladies were gathered to the citadel of Susa the capital into the custody of Hegai, that Esther was taken to the king's palace into the custody of Hegai, who was in charge of the women.*

Coercion possibly may have been involved. Esther *was taken to the king's palace and placed into the custody of Hegai* (Esth. 2:8). The others *were gathered to the citadel of Susa* (Esth. 2:8). Although we cannot be dogmatic, the original language indicates that Esther and the other women are forced to participate under the king's mandate. Esther appears to be at the mercy of a pagan king and swept along by circumstances beyond her control. Because the marriage and sexual practices of the Persian court are very different from God's holy intentions for marriage, Esther would not likely willingly place herself in a compromising situation. Nor will her cousin Mordecai allow her to pursue a path that might lead to the possibility of intermarriage outside of her Jewish nationality.

Some Bible teachers believe that Mordecai willingly places Esther in harm's way and basically signs her up as a participant in this sort of beauty pageant. Some even suggest that he is motivated by his own political ambitions and is willing to subject Esther to a life sentence in the palace, either as the next queen or as a concubine in the king's harem. That presents some difficult questions. Is doing wrong ever right? Does God allow the end to justify the means? Does God bless Mordecai's disobedience? While these are difficult questions that we cannot answer, we *do* know that God does not ever lead us on a path that is contrary to His revealed will. While He will restore His children after repentance and restitution have been made, He certainly never is the author of sin nor does He approve of disobedience. James 1:13b says, *God cannot be tempted by evil, and He Himself does not tempt anyone.* We also know that He never justifies sinful methods even if they result in a right conclusion.

Although the name of God is not mentioned in the Book of Esther, the hand of God is quite evident. Esther rests in the knowledge of God's sovereignty in the midst of an impossible situation. A chance to become the most powerful woman in the Medo-Persian Empire causes the other women to employ every technique available to gain an advantage. This is an all-out competition with no holds barred. Not much imagination is required to conjure up the type of competitive spirit that is aroused among the majority of the girls. The winner will become the next queen of Persia, with all the royal benefits the title entails. Imagine the cat fights and the temper tantrums that Esther witnesses. Petty rivalries, envy, and jealousy are commonplace. Prestige and power are the prizes for those so motivated; the stakes are high. These women have access to exquisitely embroidered garments, designer jewels, costly cosmetics, expensive oils, and priceless perfumes to entice the lonely king to choose one of them for his next queen. In a place where women hone their seductive, feminine wiles in the hopes of winning the heart of the lonely king, Esther's inner beauty shines brightly.

Esther finds herself surrounded by people concerned with the shape of their bodies or the beauty of their faces. All emphasis is on outer beauty, with little or no thought given to character or inner beauty. This sounds like the world in which we live, doesn't it? The opulent world into which Esther is swept resembles our world. Her world is obsessed with wealth, power, prestige, youth, and beauty. Sadly, in the last 2,500 years not much has changed.

Even in this ungodly and heathen environment, the character of Esther radiates through her outer beauty. Esther is distinctly different from the other women. She is a model of grace. Esther's inner strength of character and her commitment to God radiate through her face and illuminates her countenance. The hand of God is on Esther and she *found favor* (Esth. 2:9) with Hegai, the king's eunuch. He gave her *seven choice maids from the king's palace and transferred her and her maids to the best place in the harem.* Apparently various degrees of honor are present in the harem. From the beginning Esther is favored.

Maintaining any semblance of emotional balance or spiritual equilibrium in the midst of this den of iniquity is difficult for Esther. Living in the degradation of the fleshly environment of the king's harem, Esther's true beauty emerges. Here, where external beauty is the only criteria for worth or value, Esther's grace shows forth like a glittering diamond laid against a backdrop of black velvet.

As a Jew in the harem, Esther certainly is in the minority. Her people have been brought to this land as captives—as spoils of war. Anti-Semitic feelings run high. *Esther did not make known her people or her kindred, for Mordecai had instructed her that she should not make them known* (Esth. 2:10). Esther heeds his counsel.

Every day Mordecai walked back and forth in front of the court of the harem to learn how Esther was and how she fared (Esth. 2:11). Again, the text implies Esther is forced to participate in the king's search for a new queen. Mordecai is concerned for her well-being and regularly checks on her. Previously, she lives an obscure and sheltered life. Esther ekes out a meager living and makes a suitable home for herself and her cousin. As the search begins her obvious beauty catches the eye of the king's overseers. Suddenly Esther is swept into the opulent palace life as a possible candidate for the next queen. Mordecai has reason to be concerned.

Esther understands her greatest asset is not her physical beauty; it is her inner beauty. We want to learn this lesson from her. Outer beauty fades rapidly. What age and disease does not destroy, gravity distorts! Caring for the physical body is important, but developing personal holiness remains our highest priority.

**1. Read 2 Corinthians 4:16-18. What is happening to the physical body?

_____

The inner man is being renewed. How is the inner man renewed day by day?

_____

What is the definition of _temporal things_?

_____

What is the definition of _eternal things_?

_____

Are you investing in personal holiness?

_____

Spiritual maturity is gained when the inner man is renewed by the Word of God. The physical body is deteriorating. We have little control over that. We can use makeup, hair gel, self-tanner, and any number of beauty products to camouflage the worst flaws, but eventually the decreasing production of collagen will reveal the aging process. A better investment of time and energy is grooming the inner beauty of holiness. That produces dividends in this life and eternal reward in the next.

Esther is busy grooming her inner beauty, while the women around her groom themselves with exotic lotions and perfumed oils. While the women in the harem trust in cosmetology, Esther trusts in the God of Abraham, Isaac, and Jacob.

Weekly Summary

Please record insights gleaned from this week's study.

A Beauty Regime

Read Esther 1:1-23

I am in the maintenance stage of my life. I am not trying to look better; I am trying to hold my own. Frankly, this is a very costly phase. It requires the involvement of a troop of people. I have a hairstylist, a manicurist, a pedicurist, an allergist, a dermatologist, and someone who tortures me with hot wax to ensure I avoid a unibrow! Maintenance is not easy; it certainly is not cheap.

Recently I was to be interviewed on a local television program about Bible-based mothering. In preparation I visited a makeup artist to get a new look. I told you maintenance is not cheap! Anyway, I left the store with my bag containing new makeup and a bottle of self-tanner. I had been assured that a spritz of the tanner would ensure a healthy glow. Who in her right mind does not want a healthy glow, especially if the person is about to be interviewed on live television? The interview was on Monday. On Saturday night I sprayed self-tanner on my arms, my hands, and my neck. Several hours later I checked; I saw no noticeable change. A second application seemed reasonable. So again I sprayed my arms, hands, and neck. I went to bed knowing I would awake to a healthy glow.

Sunday morning I awakened early to prepare for church. Before I turned on the light I could tell I was in trouble. In my dimly lit bedroom I could see I had a healthy glow. In fact, I was glowing in the dark! Frantically I ran into the bathroom and looked in the mirror. During the night as I slept in peaceful bliss, a dye the color of dark chocolate had unevenly stained my arms and neck. Words fail me as I try to describe myself. The double dose had rendered my arms about six shades darker than my natural color. I was mottled and speckled, especially on my hands.

In a panic I sat in front of my bathroom cabinet and tried every product I had. At this point I could tell you not to try this at home. No one in her right mind would suggest doing what I did, but I was desperate. I grabbed my facial exfoliator and attempted to remove the hideous stain. It did not work. With no success I tried mascara remover. I used hydrogen peroxide, but the tanner did not budge. I moved from my bathroom cabinet to my kitchen pantry. Baking soda seemed as though it was a reasonable product to try. After all, it works wonders cleaning stubborn stains on all sorts of surfaces. I decided to try it on my skin. When this product failed, I tried lemon juice and salt. The burning sensation convinced me the concoction was working; it was not.

By this point I was panicked; my head felt faint. I left the kitchen pantry and moved into my laundry room, where I spied laundry detergent with bleach. Surely this was the ticket. Failure struck again. I almost hate to tell you what I did next. The prospect of being on live television pushed me to do something that I knew was not wise. I picked up a can of powdered bathroom cleanser! That's right. I did it. I sprinkled the noxious powder on my hands and scrubbed with a brush. You heard me. A brush. I used a brush on my hands. By now I was mentally making plans to drive to my dermatologist's office as soon as the interview was over. I expected whelps and boils to break out on my hands. They did not, but neither did the self-tanner relent. This product was powerful stuff and seriously committed to staying on my skin. Exhausted I sat down and lathered my hands in moisturizer. I promised my hands I would never put them through that again. Self-tanner is dead to me.

All I could do was wait for the botched self-tanner to fade. Monday morning arrived. I had determined to wear a long-sleeved jacket. My neck, which had only received one light application, was not horribly noticeable. But my hands were hopelessly stained. Since gloves were out of the question, I had nothing to do but go to the interview. I would attempt to be incredibly charming so no one would look at my hands! Maintenance is an expensive proposition. Beauty is pain.

Bible scholars tell us that as many as 400 young virgins may have been involved in the king's search for a new queen. In the Bible story Esther and the women in the harem are put through an extensive beauty program. A year is given over to beauty treatments. The women are indulged and pampered with spa treatments. They are taught to apply cosmetics. They learn to walk properly and to dress to accentuate their natural assets. Before they are presented to the king, the women are trained in seduction.

Years ago Craig, the boys, and I took a mission trip to the Navajo Indian Reservation in Arizona. Because we had no shower facilities at the campgrounds at which our group stayed, we drove into town and borrowed the high-school's gym dressing- room facilities. All the women and girls would drive in first to shower and do hair and makeup. After we were finished, the guys would drive over to get showered and shaved. Of course no hot water was ever left for them! My husband often laughed about the mixture of fragrances that lingered. A cloud of hairspray, mousse, gel, shampoo, conditioner, bath oil, shower gel, perfumes, powder, and cologne still emanated from the locker room long after the women were gone!

I can only imagine the smells that radiate from the palace during the year-long beautification regimes. The heavy fragrance of perfumes and oils must waft through the air and hang like a thick fog outside the harem. The emphasis among the women is on physical beauty; no expense is spared to impress the king. Every woman with the exception of Esther vies for the king's affection.

Esther is an excellent example of a woman of worth. Her life does not revolve around her physical appearance. Esther's driving ambition is not to win over the king's heart and be crowned the next queen. She is confidently resting in the sovereignty of God. She trusts Him to work in her life for her good and His glory. So great is her virtue and inner beauty, it outshines her obvious outer loveliness and physical features.

The competition among the women in the harem produces rivalries and petty jealousy. The atmosphere is hardly conducive to cultivate character when the shape of the body and the beauty of the face are the only concerns. Surrounded by catfights, competitiveness, and carnality, Esther manages to emerge as a woman of dignity and grace. The beauty of holiness in Esther's life springs forth from a heart that was fixed on God.

The contest involves much more than a beauty review; it includes a night with King Ahasuerus. The woman of his choosing will become his wife and the next queen of Persia. All other candidates will be sent to live in his harem (Esth. 2:14). The women will not be allowed to return to their families. Their purity will have been sacrificed to the sexual appetite of the king. The king is interested in outer beauty and sexual prowess. This custom is common among the monarchy of the time, but the practice is outrageous and contrary to God's holy standard of matrimony.

1. In Genesis 2:24 God revealed His plan for marriage. Read this verse. What is God's plan?

God has never intended for men to take multiple wives or concubines. This practice is culturally accepted in the Old Testament and even practiced by some of the patriarchs. However, God neither condones nor endorses it.

We live in a society that measures a woman's worth by her external appearance and her ability to accent her assets and camouflage her flaws. Appearance is more desirable than is character or the condition of the heart. First Samuel 16:7 says, *Man looks at the outward appearance, but the Lord looks at the heart*. Outer beauty may be people's standard, but God is interested in the condition of the heart. Beloved, do not compromise or become conformed to the image of this world. Its standards are contrary to those of our King.

A Queen Crowned

Read Esther 2: 1-23

Can you imagine? Twelve months of pampering and spa treatments. No cooking. No cleaning. No carpool. The only thing on every woman's mind is to win the contest and claim the crown. Every woman is fixated on appearance—every woman, that is, except Esther. Esther is reluctant to participate. From the text she apparently has been forced into the harem against her will. However, to her credit, she faces an unspeakable circumstance with grace and dignity. I believe she senses God's hand in her situation and prepares to trust in Him.

King Ahasuerus spares no expense to prepare the women of his harem. After 12 months of beauty treatments each woman will go to the king. She will be allowed to take anything she desires that might possibly enhance her chances of winning the title of queen of Persia. After spending the night in the king's bed, the woman will return to the harem of concubines. She will not be permitted to leave the harem to marry or return to her family. She will not see the king again unless he specifically asks for her. Any children conceived of their union will be reared to serve in the court, but they will not be legitimate heirs to the throne.

Esther is taken to the king four years after Queen Vashti is deposed. *She did not request anything except what Hegai, the king's eunuch, who was in charge of the women, advised* (Esth. 2:15). She finds favor in Hegai's eyes and trusts his guidance.

Through circumstances beyond her control, Esther finds herself in an impossible situation. The text does not divulge any insight into how Esther feels about her circumstance. The writer does not make editorial comment; he presents the facts of the story without the intrusion of personal observation. In this study many of our questions will go unanswered.

While I want to avoid conjecture, I assume Esther hates her circumstances. They violate every conviction and moral principle Mordecai instills in her. She surely wonders how God can let such a horrible thing happen to her. Relying on her Jewish upbringing, I believe she trusts in the sovereignty of God and rests in His providence.

Esther finds favor in all who meet her; the king's reaction to her is no different. King Ahasuerus falls in love with Esther. Esther 2:17 says, *And the king loved Esther more than all the women, and she found favor and kindness with him more than all the virgins, so that he set the royal crown on her head and made her queen instead of Vashti.*

While we cannot fully unravel this story, we know that God causes *all things to work together for good* (Rom. 8:28). Is Esther right to submit herself to a perverse situation? Can she possibly refuse to be placed in the harem of the king even if it costs her life? Why does God allow Esther to be put in such a horrible situation? These are difficult questions that we cannot answer dogmatically. The Scripture records the story without giving us details that are necessary to draw a firm conclusion. Personally, when I cannot understand what God is doing, I simply trust Him. I know He is a good God. I know where Satan rules, God overrules. By faith, I operate on that which I do know. I do know that we see the providential purpose of Almighty God at work in Esther's life personally and in the lives of the Jews corporately.

The king crowns Esther the queen of Persia. *The king gave a great banquet, Esther's banquet, for all his princes and his servants; he also made a holiday for the provinces and gave gifts according to the king's bounty* (Esth. 2:18).

Not only does Esther have new standing in the kingdom, Mordecai is now *sitting at the king's gate* (Esth. 2:21). A wall surrounds the palace complex. Legal and civil matters are settled and commercial business is transacted in a building at the gate. Just as God has providentially placed Esther in a place of authority in the palace, He has sovereignly orchestrated a new position for Mordecai. It will help Mordecai overhear a murderous plot being hatched against the king. God definitely is at work in this event.

**1. Read Esther 2:21-23. A plot against the king is hatched by two disgruntled employees. What is their plan?

_____

The plot becomes known to Mordecai. What does he do?

_____

The culprits are caught before they can carry out their murderous deed. What happens?

_____

God is constantly at work. Be careful not to lose sight of God's sovereign dealings in your life. Busy schedules, the monotony of daily living, or spiritual dullness may cause us to become indifferent to His stirring. While we tend to focus on our own ability to garner control over our own lives, God truly is the One at work behind the scenes. The eye of faith is required to see it; the audacity of faith is required to believe it.

**2. Read Psalm 37:23-24. What does this passage teach us about God's daily involvement in our lives?

_____

What happens when we stumble in our walk with Him?

_____

We can misinterpret God's plan and purpose. Because we cannot see Him at work or sense His presence, we can reach the wrong conclusion. We surmise He is unconcerned or worse, cruel—powerless to help. Obviously the world, the flesh, and the devil induce us to doubt God. Learn this, dear mom: the immortal, invisible, all-wise, unseen God is at work. His silence does not signal indifference. He is in control. Learn to walk by faith; rest in that glorious truth.

Silently and seamlessly God is at work. Psalm 118:23 says, _This is the Lord's doing; it is marvelous in our eyes_. Even when we cannot unravel the mysteries of life, we can rest in Him. Remember, He has an eternal perspective. He is not in a hurry. He is not constrained by time as we know it. Compared to our maddening schedules, God is extremely deliberate and painfully slow. He is working His divine plan and purpose in our lives. He is not as concerned about making us happy as He is about making us holy. Trust me, this is a long slow process!

God's plans are not hindered by the secular world. His purposes can override the godless environment of the Persian court in Esther's day and the ungodly of ours. To doubt that is to limit His power and draw human parameters around His sovereign control. God is never constrained by our sphere of limited knowledge. His purposes and plans are much larger than is our comprehension. He is everpresent and always working in the details of His humanity.

3. God is a good God. Satan wants you to think otherwise. Refuse his lies and trust in God's revelation of Himself. Read Psalm 84:11. What does the psalmist teach us about our God?

_____

Don't let your life experiences cause you to limit God's work in your life. Your past may have led you to develop a crooked concept of God. Look to the Bible for an accurate picture of God; trust in the truth of His Word.

4. God is working together in the circumstances of our lives for our good and His glory. Read James 1:17. What is the source of every good gift?

_____

In this verse how does James describe God?

_____

In Him _is no variation or shifting shadow_. What does that mean to you personally?

_____

Whether you can see His hand or sense His presence, He is at work in your life at this very moment. God has a way of moving silently but surely. He specializes in turning the mundane into the miraculous. Learn to keep your eyes on Jesus and trust in Him, regardless of the world situation or the circumstances of our lives. God is at work, though the eye of faith is necessary to realize it. Just wait and see!

A Woman of Worth

Read Assorted Passages

Esther is the new reigning queen of the Medo-Persian Empire. This young woman, probably no more than 20-years old, has been made queen instead of Vashti (Esth. 2:17). Esther, an orphan who lives in exile in a foreign land as a trophy of war, is now exalted to the highest position a woman could hold in all the land. A Jew in the midst of a growing anti-Semitic climate, Esther—obeying the counsel of her beloved cousin—continues to keep her nationality hidden.

Using my sanctified imagination I can see Esther, God's star, in the royal court. As the queen of Persia she now sits on the throne with dignity and grace. Shiny black curls tumble down her back; silver combs pin them up on each side. She is poised and regal in her carriage. This characteristic emanates from her inner strength. Her crown is heavy and a bit cumbersome. It requires her to hold her chin upward to balance the weight. The queen's crown is studded with rubies and emeralds. She wears a golden necklace with a large, solitary diamond. Its heavy chain emphasizes her swan-like neck and magnifies her lovely skin. Her magnificent beauty is further enhanced by her royal wardrobe. Threads of gold and silver are interwoven into her gilded gown. As she sits on the throne, heavy fabrics of her regal gown gather in pleats and folds about her tiny frame. Her feet are hidden from view but she wears porpoise-skin sandals encrusted with jewels and tied with tasseled metallic cords. The royal crest of the Persian monarchy is emblazoned on the back of her magnificent robe. As she walks, it creates a flowing train. The weight of it would overtake the petite queen were it not for the handful of attendants that assist her. With each step the queen takes, servants lift the robe. This causes it to billow out behind her. Esther has traded a life of poverty for the king's wealth, her weakness for his strength, her bankruptcy for all the glories and riches of the kingdom.

What strong imagery her transformation evokes in the heart and mind of a Christian! We too have traded our poverty for Christ's wealth. Paul writes, *For you know the grace of our Lord Jesus Christ, that though He was rich, yet for your sake He became poor, so that you through His poverty might become rich* (2 Cor. 8:9). We traded sinful wretchedness for His righteousness. Second Corinthians 5:21 says, *He made Him who knew no sin to be sin on our behalf, that we might become the righteousness of God in Him.* We were wandering in darkness. We were bound by sin, Satan, and self. We were dead in trespasses and sins but God was rich in mercy, because of His great love with which He loved us. By grace through faith He made us alive together with Christ (see Eph. 2:1-5). We have been given royal standing in the family of God. Christ has made us to be *heirs of God and fellow heirs with Christ* (Rom. 8:17). We have been made heirs of God. Imagine that! Galatians 4:7 says, *Therefore you are no longer a slave, but a son; and if a son, then an heir through God.* God is our Father and Jesus Christ is our brother in the faith.

Like Esther, we have been called to live in newness of life—to experience the fullness of the life of Christ in us. We glory in His grace and mercy. You and I have been crowned as queens in the royal household of God. Now we are faced with learning to live like it!

Esther knew the true beauty secrets of a woman of God. Rather than using a heavy hand with cosmetic enhancements, Esther's radiance is the result of personal holiness. Psalm 34:5 says, *They looked to Him and were radiant, and their faces will never be ashamed.* Her fragrance was the presence of the Lord God in her life. Second Corinthians 2:14 says, *But thanks be to God, who always leads us in His triumph in Christ, and manifests through us the sweet aroma of the knowledge of Him in every place.*

While we certainly have the right and the option to use every cosmetic product available to enhance our appearance, we can resolutely refuse to rely on the world's manufactured merchandise. No cosmetic that people make can possibly produce the winsome beauty of a woman captured by the love of God. Nothing is as lovely as the adornment of Christ in a woman (or a man). Nothing makes a woman more appealing or more alluring than the power of God resting confidently on her. Esther displays a radiant grace and dignity coupled with an air of authenticity in the midst of unparalleled extravagance and unmatched sensuality. Everyone takes notice!

While Esther's outward appearance is enhanced by the application of fragrant oils and cosmetics, her inward beauty radiates forth from her surrendered spirit. Psalm 45:13 says, *The King's daughter is all glorious within; her clothing is interwoven with gold.* Godliness is the ornamentation of beauty—the perfect accessory for a Christian woman! First Peter 3:3-4 echoes this truth: It says, *Your adornment must not be merely external—braiding the hair, and wearing gold jewelry, or putting on dresses; but let it be the hidden person of the heart, with the imperishable quality of a gentle and quiet spirit, which is precious in the sight of God.*

Outer beauty will fade. Inner beauty, cultivated by the Word of God, grows more radiant with time. When the emphasis is solely on outer beauty, the latter years will be miserable. The inevitable laugh lines, crow's feet, and wrinkles that accompany aging will serve as silent reminders of the decaying effects of time. The best beauty secret in the world is to love Jesus Christ with all your heart, soul, and mind. It cannot be bottled and cannot be bought!

Proverbs 31:10-31 gives us a thumbnail sketch of a virtuous woman. Her value is not found in her outer beauty. Her physical attributes are not even mentioned. Her worth is based on her relationship with the Lord. The virtuous woman honors her husband, cherishes her children, handles her home, and cares for her community.

**1. Read Proverbs 31:10-31. Make a list of the virtues of a godly woman. Spend some time meditating on the character qualities of a godly woman.

relationship with husband
relationship with children
relationship with home
relationship with community

What areas could use improvement?

_____

_____

Turn your evaluation of your spiritual life into a prayer. Ask God to help you improve the weak areas and further develop your strengths. May the desire and prayer of your heart be to become a virtuous woman whose *worth is far above jewels* (Prov. 31:10).

According to the Scripture, a godly woman is proficient, trustworthy, strong, faithful, energetic, sensitive, confident, organized, intelligent, conscientious, creative, compassionate, respected, wise, resourceful, gracious, poised, secure, gentle, kind, and courageous. Her strength of character is a byproduct of her walk with God.

Jesus is the best beauty secret in the whole world. No ointment, no oil, no fragrance, no cosmetic, no cologne, and no cream can compete with the beauty of Christ expressed in the life of a Christian. Acts 4:13 says, *Now as they observed the confidence of Peter and John, and understood that they were uneducated and untrained men, they were amazed, and began to recognize them as having been with Jesus.* A heart that is wholly His makes a winsome disciple. A quiet strength and dignity rests on the one who has given his/her life to Christ and endeavors to live by His holy standard. Regardless of the carnal environment, the crassness of the crowd, or the ungodly circumstances that your pilgrim's path may force you to pass through (for some it will be unsaved family members, for some it will be the job, for some it will be the neighborhood), the love of God sets you apart. Others will sense the aroma of Christ on your life and the adornment of a heart surrendered to Him. When you are walking with the Lord, others will sense you have been with Jesus.

As we endeavor to learn to live like queens, we will discover true beauty radiates from the life of Christ. A will that is tender to the promptings of the Holy Spirit is reflected in a radiant countenance. A yielded life produces the fragrant aroma of Christ. Like Esther, we do not rely on the trappings of this world for our beauty. Through a relationship with the Lord Jesus we cultivate the beauty of holiness.

A Cruel Character

Read Esther 3:1-15

Recently Craig and I had the joyous privilege of slipping away for the weekend. We indulged ourselves in the extravagant luxury of Peacock Hill outside Franklin, TN. Beautiful furnishings, luxurious fabrics, and comfortable surroundings make this pre-Civil War inn charming and inviting. Peacock Hill, a working farm, is so-named because of the hordes of wild peacocks that frequently make it their home.

Peacock Hill is beautifully situated among the rolling hills of the Cumberland Plateau; this gives it an exceptionally lovely setting. Once we were settled into our room, I stepped outside to take some pictures of the picturesque surroundings. I promptly discovered I had locked myself out of my room. Heading to the front desk for another key, I ran onto a rather comical but unsettling sight. A male peacock was violently attacking the chrome bumper of our truck! In stunned silence I watched the spectacle. The peacock would back away from our truck, use his magnificent plumage for balance, and frantically claw with his exposed talons at his own reflection in the shiny bumper. All the while he was pecking his image and shrieking loudly. He had opened a wound on his leg from his vicious and repeated assaults on our bumper. Blood began to splatter the hood of our truck as I watched in amazement. I then found the source of his exhibition. A peahen was watching his behavior. A look of great disdain and disgust showed on her face. When I called the innkeeper, I was informed that mating season had arrived on the farm. The male was fighting his imaginary rival suitor for the honor of his lady friend!

For the duration of our stay the innkeeper taped towels over our bumper. They served to dissuade our peacock friend from sparring with our vehicle. The owners called the vet for advice. He was informed them that the peacock would need to be put up in the barn lest he fight to the death for his ladylove!

In the midst of our lovely weekend something went awry with the peacocks that threatened to spoil our rest and relaxation. As you read this chapter in Esther's life, you will notice something goes terribly wrong and threatens her very existence. Esther 3:1 says, *King Ahasuerus promoted Haman, the son of Hammedatha the Agagite, and advanced him and established his authority over all the princes who were with him.* Just as Esther settles into a blissful state of contentment, evil raises its ugly head.

Before we proceed, here is a brief history lesson. God instructs Saul to utterly destroy the Amalekites. In 1 Samuel 15:3 God says, *"Now go and strike Amalek and utterly destroy all that he has, and do not spare him; but put to death both man and woman, child and infant, ox and sheep, camel and donkey."*

**1. God gives very specific instructions to Saul. Read 1 Samuel 15:8-9. What do Saul and the people do?

_____

Read 1 Samuel 15:10-23. What does Saul tell Samuel about the mission?

_____

What does Samuel hear that makes him question Saul's truthfulness?

_____

Caught in his lie, how does Saul attempt to shift the blame?

_____

Samuel declares God is not interested in sheep and oxen. What is He after?

_____

How does God view rebellion?

_____

What is the consequence of Saul's rebellion?

_____

Partial obedience is disobedience. Generations later the sin of Saul still has consequences.

Moms, instruct your children to obey you promptly and completely. Teach them that partial obedience is the same as disobedience. Do not accept incomplete or delayed obedience. Help your children to obey. If necessary, take them firmly but gently by the arm and help them obey. Teach them the serious consequences of disobedience. As God's ambassador in the home, help them understand the importance of immediate obedience. Learning to obey authority is a vital life lesson that is best learned at home. Start early. This principle of parenting will take you a good 20 years to teach them, so don't get discouraged!

Now, back to Esther. Mordecai overhears two men discussing a plot to assassinate the king. He tells Esther; *she informed the king in Mordecai's name* (Esth. 2:22). Justice occurs swiftly. The two men are investigated, convicted, and hanged on a gallows. This grisly scene is designed to strike fear in the king's subjects.

Mordecai's quick action saves the life of the king. Mordecai is the hero of this story. We assume Mordecai will receive a public commendation and a promotion. That is not what happens. *After these events King Ahasuerus promoted Haman . . . and advanced him and established his authority over all the princes who were with him* (Esth. 3:1). Interesting. Mordecai saves the king's life, but Haman gets the promotion. King Ahasuerus has a lapse in judgment when he advances Haman. Haman is a cruel character. Mordecai is the one who has saved the king from assassination. Surely he is a more worthy candidate for promotion than Haman is. This doesn't seem fair, does it? Beloved mom, learn this. Life is not always fair.

Moms, teach your children this lesson—life is not fair! Life is just not fair! Get over it! Get used to it! From your child's earliest days, he/she will blurt out, "That's not fair." Reply to your little progeny, "You are so right. Life is not fair." Acknowledge it. Commiserate with them, but help them get past the disenchantment and move on. Do not allow a disappointment—even a big one—to become a life-defining moment for your child (or yourself). The child of God is defined by his/her relationship with Christ. Sorrow and discontent are bound to touch every person's life. Only the believer can embrace the sorrow, grieve the hurt, get God's perspective, receive His healing, and move on past it. Use these teachable moments to help your child understand that life is not designed to be fair. God Himself is not fair. If He were fair, He would give us what we deserve, which is hell. Instead He opts to be just instead. God sent His only Son to die in our place and pay our sin debt. That was not fair; that was merciful. That was grace!

Life is not fair. Mordecai should get the promotion; Haman does instead. Haman is an Agagite. He is a descendant of the Amalekites, the perpetual enemies of the Jews. Does that name ring a bell? Do you remember studying Israel's history with the Amalekites? If Saul had done what he had been commanded to do, years later the Jews would not be facing extermination at the hand of Haman. Saul's failure to exterminate the Amalekites jeopardizes the survival of the Jewish line.

Moms, surely you did not miss the message of Saul's failure. When Saul fails to do what God instructs him to do, this costs him the throne. Moses is another man whose disobedience is costly. Moses' failure prevents him from going into the Promised Land. These men miss out on God's best for their lives because of their foolish disobedience. They cheat themselves out of God's blessings. That is bad, but that is certainly not the worst part. Saul's sin puts his descendants in peril. How is that for a scary thought? When we disobey God, we will surely suffer for our sin. However, our children and our children's children may bear the pain of our toolhardy failure. Generations later the effects of our sin may still linger and produce pain and heartache in innocent lives. We are compelled to live lives of personal holiness and practical righteousness as we hand our faith down to our children and hopefully influence many generations for righteousness.

2. Look up Psalm 112:1-2. What does this passage teach us?

_____

What are some practical ways we can influence our children and our children's children for the cause of Christ?

As our children move into the adult world, they will pass from under our authority. Authority is temporary; our godly influence is permanent. Righteousness endures forever.

Esther lives in a time much like the culture in which we live. Evil seems to be overtaking righteousness. Just as in Esther's day, life is tough. Life is not fair. Beloved mom, take comfort in the Lord. In the midst of difficult circumstances He is silently engaged in the daily grind of our lives. With relentless patience and purpose He works out His plans and His purposes.

A queen knows how to stand and strike a regal pose. As members of the heavenly monarchy we stand on the promises of God. A queen knows how to walk properly. As members of the royal family we walk by faith.

A Servant of Satan

Read Esther 3:1-15

René Smith is one of my dear friends. Her son, Brandon, recently married. I asked whether I could slip into the bride's room while the girls were getting ready and take some candid pictures. The flower girl, Hannah Smith, was an adorable 5-year old. I found her with electric rollers in her hair and about to put on her white satin dress covered with gossamer layers of chiffon. A floral wreath for her hair, dainty ballet slippers, and a basket of rose petals would complete the ensemble of this adorable angel. At the last moment her mom, Joanna, took the rollers out of her hair. Hannah winced. "That hurts," she declared firmly. "Honey, take it from me," I empathized. "Beauty is pain—something you have to get used to!"

Ain't that the truth? Let's face it. Life is difficult and full of pain. Moms, teach your children this valuable lesson. We live in the midst of a sin-cursed world; we will all suffer for it. Bad things happen to good people. Worse yet, good things happen to bad people. This life lesson does not seem fair, but it nonetheless is a reality. Those of us who know the Lord do not attempt to unravel the mysteries of this life. Rather, we endeavor to walk by faith with our eyes on Jesus Christ. If you are to live like a queen, learn to walk by faith in Jesus.

Esther's royal life is rife with problems. We assume this Jew in unfriendly territory has been brought to the king's harem against her will. She has been held there for a year before being named the queen of Persia. I believe she is resting in God's providence and sovereignty, but her life is anything but easy. Now she is forced to wrestle with the king's slight of her cousin Mordecai, who has saved the king's life. Esther and Mordecai assume he will be exalted to the king's right hand. Surely he will have some sway in bettering the treatment of the Jews in the Medo-Persian Empire. Perhaps Mordecai might be the deliverer who, like Moses, would exact freedom for God's enslaved people. But Haman is promoted. *All the king's servants who are at the king's gate bowed down and paid homage to Haman; for so the king had commanded concerning him* (Esth. 3:2). Promoted and proud—a dangerous combination in Haman's wicked heart.

According to the king's decree, all the men except Mordecai bow to Haman. He neither *bowed down nor paid homage* (Esth. 3:2b). The king's servants are stunned by Mordecai's blatant rebellion. *"Why are you transgressing the king's command?"* (Esth. 3:3) they query. Mordecai replies, "I am a Jew." As a follower of Jehovah God he is duty-bound to bow to no one. They promptly report to Haman about Mordecai's heritage.

Here I interject a bit of mothering advice without taking away from the seriousness of the subject. The king's servants *tattle* on Mordecai. Tattling is one of those annoying habits of little children. Discourage tattling unless a child is in danger of injury. Proverbs 26:17 says, *Like one who takes a dog by the ears is he who passes by and meddles with strife not belonging to him.* Teach your children to play nicely and mind their own business! No tattling.

Children delight to draw us into their petty arguments in an attempt to make us judge and jury. So here is a little motherly advice for you. If possible try to avoid getting sucked into these childish disagreements. If possible let your children settle their own arguments. Children need to learn to defer to the desires of another. This is an important social skill and is best learned at home. If you cannot avoid adjudicating a disagreement, remember every argument has two sides. Before you render a judgment, make sure you have all the facts.

As a young mom, as my boys played I tried to stay within earshot. When squabbles arose, I tried to let them settle their differences. My mantra was, "Work it out with words." If they could settle the argument without any bloodletting, I did not intervene. However, if tempers began to escalate, I moved in and tried to mediate. Even when our children played, we did not allow the boys to fight or wrestle with each other. (I am not saying they never did— just saying we did not allow it!) They have always been big boys; I knew someone would end up hurt! Third, I did not allow tattling. I tried to teach the boys not to tattle unless someone was in danger.

**1. Read Proverbs 18:17. What can you learn from this verse?

_____

How can you apply it to your arsenal of mothering skills?

_____

Children have a way of skewing the facts in their favor. That is why they tattle on each other and race to be the first to tell their story. I knew that whoever got to me first wanted to force me into a judgment call without my hearing the whole story. Teach your child to settle his/her own disputes. Model this behavior for them. Mediate if necessary, but put on them the burden of learning this important life skill. Learning to show deference is difficult, especially for young children, but this is a very important social skill that will serve them throughout their lives. This lesson is not easily learned. For about 20 years it will be a work in progress.

Now, back to Esther. The men reveal to Haman Mordecai's ethnicity. How does that go over? *Haman was filled with rage* (Esth. 3:5). Cue scary music. This can't be good! Satan uses Haman's unrestrained anger toward Mordecai as the breeding ground to hatch a plan that will lead to the destruction of the Jewish race. A queen must know who her enemies are. Satan is a very real enemy. Learn his tactics.

Weekly Summary

Please record insights gleaned from this week's study.

A Sinister Minister

Read Esther 3:1-15

The peacock incident at Peacock Hill was not our only animal encounter. Peacock Hill is a 1,000-acre working cattle farm. Like most farms it has an eclectic collection of animals. Besides the wild peacocks, cows, horses, cats, and dogs wander the property. All this adds to its authenticity and country charm.

Craig and I enjoy strolling the property and taking in the sights. I am an avid amateur photographer, so I rarely am without my camera. On one such outing we noticed the owner's 6-year-old grandson with two pet goats in a pen. Hoping for a photo-op, I asked whether we could pet the goats. The child assured us they were friendly and invited us to join him. Craig and I opened the latch and went in to meet them. One goat was quite aloof, but the other was thrilled at the attention. As I snapped away, Craig rubbed the head and neck of the goat. The goat affectionately rubbed against Craig's leg, lifted his head, and begged for more. Carefully framing each photo, I was pleased with the shots I was capturing of Craig interacting with the farm animals. In much the same way a faithful dog would, this goat was begging Craig for more attention. He was walking in figure-eight patterns around Craig's feet, looking up at him adoringly, and tenderly leaning against him. *This is so cute*, I thought as I clicked away with my camera.

With my camera still at my eye, I was startled to see this docile, gentle goat back up, lower his head—complete with horns——and prepare to ram my husband! Craig instinctively caught the goat by the horns and prevented the intended blow from landing. The goat backed up and proceeded to attempt another strike. As he exited the pen, the grandson assured us the goat had never before acted this way. Once again my husband grabbed the goat by the horns and this time did not let go of the ornery animal. My husband suddenly found himself and this goat engaged in some sort of dance around the pasture. Craig held firmly to the horns while the goat continued to attempt to butt!

Now I would love to tell you that I bravely ran to my husband's aid and helped free him from this tyrannical goat, but I could not stop laughing long enough to be of much help! In my defense, Craig also thought it was very funny, but he was not sure how he was going to turn loose of this determined animal. I did try to take a picture of this comical scene to preserve this memory forever, but I could not hold the camera steady. Instead, I ran to the gate and held it open for my husband, who was still struggling to free himself from Billy Goat Gruff. I plucked a handful of grass and clover, ran outside the pen, and called the goat. To our utter amazement, he timidly trotted to the fence and began to nibble the grass out of my hand while Craig escaped the goat pen!

That goat had *two sides* to his personality. He could be charming and affectionate one moment and antagonistic and aggressive the next. People often are like that. They learn to modify their behavior according to the need of the moment, but they may turn on you at any time. James 1:8 says that *a double-minded man* (is) *unstable in all his ways.*

Haman is a man of similar disposition. In the presence of the king he is articulate, efficient, and eloquent. These qualities serve Haman well and probably lead to his promotion as prime minister. But Haman has another side. Anger and murderous rage are hidden in his heart's seamy side which the king does not see. Satan is easily able to introduce his sadistic plan to annihilate the Jews into the brutal mind of Haman. Haman's heart is a cesspool of violence waiting to be exploited.

Satan uses unbelievers to accomplish his fiendish plans. He is *the god of this world* and he *has blinded the minds of the unbelieving* (2 Cor. 4:4). Unbelievers are held captive under the sway of the devil. He can oppress unbelievers and actually can possess them. He can use them, wittingly or unwittingly, to perform his purposes. Satan can suggest evil thoughts that appeal to the corrupt heart. When the natural propensity to do evil cooperates with the wicked suggestion, Satan's plans are pressed into action. Satan tempts Haman to accomplish his fiendish plan. Since the tempting thought aligns with his anti-Semitic belief system, Haman is a willing pawn in Satan's scheme to destroy the line of the Messiah.

Satan cannot possess a child of God, but he can oppress believers. Satan has the ability to plant thoughts in the minds of believers. Although God sets the boundaries, Satan is allowed to tempt us to sin by planting thoughts and ideas into our minds. If we have not faithfully renewed our minds with the Word of God, we will fall prey to his deceptive schemes. When we are in the process of learning God's Word through comprehensive, in-depth study, we can recognize Satan's lies, combat them with the truth of God's Word, put them to death, and walk in victory.

**1. To more fully understand how Satan assaults us and entices us to sin, read James 1:13-15. What is the progression of sin from the thought to the behavior?

_____

How can you short-circuit Satan's enticements?

_____

At the moment of conversion the blessed Holy Spirit of God moves into your quickened human spirit. Your name is written in the Lamb's Book of Life. Your sins are forgiven. You no longer are sentenced to hell. Heaven becomes your eternal home. These are just some of the glorious events which take place instantaneously. However, you bring an unregenerate mind into your new birth. Practically speaking, you operate with the same thought process after conversion as you did before it. Knowledge of the things of God is not automatic at the moment of conversion. God does not implant a microchip of divine knowledge of the truth. You are compelled to renew your minds through the study of the Word. Otherwise your mind remains imprinted with habit patterns and sinful practices from the past.

Only through the in-depth study of the Word of God can you replace the lies of the enemy with the truth. If you do not strive to renew your mind with the truth of God's Word, you are bound to operate with the deeply entrenched habit patterns from your unregenerate past. Until the destructive thought patterns of the past are replaced with the truth, you will be handicapped in your Christian walk. You will be attempting to live the new life with old methods. Mixing the old methods with the new life in Christ will not work!

2. In Matthew 9:16-17 Jesus explains this principle. Read these verses and record your insight.

_____

When you became a Christian, the Lord did not merely patch up the old; He makes all things new. At the moment of your conversion you become a new creation (2 Cor. 5:17). Second Corinthians 5:17 says, _Therefore if anyone is in Christ, he is a new creature; the old things passed away; behold, new things have come._ Positionally at the moment of conversion you receive the mind of Christ. To make that truth a practical reality in your life, however, seek daily to renew your mind with the Word of God.

I have found reading repetitively is the best way to renew the mind. I take an extended passage of Scripture and read it over and over again for several days or even weeks. I want to renew my mind with God's Word. This process is slow and tedious. Old habit patterns left over from my life before my conversion are deeply embedded. They stubbornly resist my new life in Christ. If I only read the Word of God devotionally, I will only get a snippet of the Scripture each day. This technique is not adequate to battle the world, the flesh, and the devil successfully. I also read doctrinally and add in-depth study of the Bible to assimilate the Word of God and live accordingly. The process of sanctification is tough work. First Timothy 4:7b-8 says, _Discipline yourself for the purpose of godliness; for bodily discipline is only of little profit, but godliness is profitable for all things, since it holds promise for the present life and also for the life to come._ We apply ourselves to the study of the Word of God to experience the power of God resting on our lives. Invest in this worthy endeavor!

Haman is an evil man and a willing pawn in Satan's plan. Haman eagerly receives the devil's plan to annihilate the Jews. Once again, Satan attempts to find a man who will take care of those pesky Jews once and for all. Satan is manipulating circumstances to get his candidate, Haman, in a position of power to accomplish his dastardly deed.

Satan is always at work attempting to hinder God's purpose and plan. Satan is called *the prince of the power of the air, of the spirit that is now working in the sons of disobedience* (Eph. 2:2). Satan is the leader of the demonic forces. Paul writes, *For our struggle is not against flesh and blood, but against the rulers, against the powers, against the world forces of this darkness, against the spiritual forces of wickedness in the heavenly places* (Eph. 6:12). *Satan is a murderer from the beginning, and does not stand in the truth, because there is no truth in him. Whenever he speaks a lie, he speaks from his own nature; for he is a liar, and the father of lies* (John 8:44). Satan's power is limited, but he is a formidable foe.

In Matthew 4:1 Satan is called *the tempter*. Matthew 13:19 refers to him as *the evil one*. In Colossians 1:13 he is *the ruler of the domain of darkness*. From these Scriptures we can get an idea of the evil persona of the devil. He intends to keep his methods cloaked in darkness and mystery. The enemy is strong; his power is not to be underestimated. However, our God is immensely more powerful; Satan is a defeated foe!

A queen will identify her enemies. She will be committed to routing them. Her goal will be to protect her kingdom from the onslaught of her enemies. She will become a student of the Word to gain the advantage over her adversary. She will become a prayer warrior on behalf of her royal subjects. Looking good in the crown is just part of her royal responsibility!

A Deadly Decree

Read Esther 3:1-15

Esther has been queen for five years when Satan manipulates Haman to set his plan in motion. *Haman disdained to lay hands on Mordecai alone, for they had told him who the people of Mordecai were; therefore Haman sought to destroy all the Jews, the people of Mordecai who were throughout the whole kingdom of Ahasuerus* (Esth. 3:8).

Haman's anger at one man's snub quickly turns into a plot to extinguish the entire Jewish population. Why? Haman is an Agagite. Remember them? They hate the Jews. The Agagites are perpetual enemies of the Jews. Haman nurses a prejudice he has known since childhood.

No child is born with prejudice. Intolerance of any type is learned behavior. I cannot prove it, but I can assume that this is the life lesson Haman's parents taught him. He is acting on the behavior that has been modeled in his home. His people are prejudiced against the Jews. Haman has been taught to hate them as well. Now Haman is in a position to do something about his bigotry. Once and for all he will rid the land of the scourge of the Jews. In the process he will vindicate his ancestors and become a hero to his people.

In the first month, which is the month Nisan, in the twelfth year of King Ahasuerus, Pur, that is the lot, was cast before Haman (Esth. 3:7). Pur, as a single dice is known, is a clay cube inscribed with characters or dots. It was a common pagan practice used to consult the gods to discern days or fortunes.

As a side note, casting lots also was used by the Jews to query Yahweh. Without the full written revelation or the indwelling Holy Spirit, in the Old Testament the method was employed to gain the mind of God. The pagan world had a counterfeit practice to inquire of its gods. Learn this: Satan cannot create; he can only copy. He is not above imitating the things of God.

Haman's dice have the months and days of the year inscribed. The lots indicate the month Adar—a date 11 months in the future.

1. Read Esther 3:8-11. Haman goes to the king. How does he present his complaint about Mordecai?

_____

What does he propose be done to the Jews living in the kingdom?

_____

What is the king's response?

_____

Haman skillfully manipulates the king by bringing a veiled accusation against the Jews in general. He says, _"There is a certain people scattered and dispersed among the peoples in all the provinces of your kingdom; their laws are different from those of all other people and they do not observe the king's laws, so it is not in the king's interest to let them remain"_ (Esth. 3:8). Remember that only Mordecai has refused to bow to Haman. Only Mordecai has violated the king's command. Haman couches his concern in terms of a brewing, massive rebellion against the monarchy. Notice Haman carefully avoids mentioning the nationality of the people. Sadly, the king appears to be too unconcerned to inquire for more details.

Haman sweetens the deal. If the king signs the decree, Haman can put 10,000 talents of silver in King Ahasuerus' treasury. In their economy that is 375 tons. The king has nearly emptied his coffers on his misguided attempt to conquer Greece. The mention of money plays into the king's greed. Then, as if bored by the whole issue, the king says, _"The silver is yours, and the people also, to do with them as you please"_ (Esth. 3:11). With a wave of the hand, the king looses a holocaust on God's chosen people.

Haman disguises his personal agenda. He convinces the king the best interest of the empire is at stake. The king blindly grants Haman authority in the matter. The king fails to seek further counsel and bases his decision solely on the information that Haman provides. Since Haman's scheme is greatly influenced by his hatred for the Jews, by trusting him the king makes a grave error in judgment.

Beware of snap decisions. In an effort to mislead the child of God the enemy can misrepresent the facts. Before you make a decision, spend time in prayer. Ask God to confirm His plan and purpose to you through the Word of God. Seek wise counsel. Craig and I have sought the wise counsel of mature believers when we were faced with big decisions in our lives. God often has given us valuable insights and fresh perspectives through the biblical advice of men and women who are strong in the faith and impartial in their guidance. Seeking godly counsel is a biblical principle that cannot be overstated.

The king takes his signet ring from his hand and gives it to Haman. The signet ring bestows Haman with the full authority of the throne. In doing so the king puts his stamp of approval on Haman's heinous plan, which ultimately will include his queen.

A plan for exterminating the Jews has been drafted and put into motion. It has been sealed with the king's signet ring; it is irrevocable. The murderous plot will be carried out on the 12th month of the year. The die has been cast!

With the stroke of a pen and the imprint of the king's gold ring into hot, melted wax, unrestrained evil is unleashed on God's chosen people. Haman's wicked plan is being put into effect. As evil devours Haman's thought processes, he gives in to his wicked passions. He loosens the reins on any lingering self-restraint or moral bearings that he has retained. A holocaust, similar to the one Hitler would recreate in the 1930s, is launched. Esther 3:13-14 says, *Letters were sent by couriers to all the king's provinces to destroy, to kill, and to annihilate all the Jews, both young and old, women and children, in one day, the thirteenth day of the twelfth month, which is the month Adar, and to seize their possessions as plunder.* A copy of the edict to be issued as law in every province is published to all the peoples so that they could prepare for this day.

News of the impending destruction of the Jewish people spreads across the kingdom. The Jews begin living under the dread of the impending sentence of death legislated by Haman. The deadly date hangs over them like a gathering storm cloud. Grown men weep unashamedly; they know they will be unable to defend their families. Jewish mommas sob as they tuck their little ones into bed at night, because they know the horrible end that awaits them on the appointed day of execution. The children no longer play silly games or sing and dance in the streets. Their innocence has been stolen by the imminent calamity. Laughter no longer is heard as the trepidation of terror draws closer. It smothers the Jewish families under the weight of despair. Fear hangs in the air like a dense fog and is nearly palatable as the Israelites contemplate their bleak future.

An assault on God's covenant people at any time really is an assault on the authority, power, and character of God. The name of *God* is not mentioned in the Book of Esther, but the power of His presence is evident. *Satan* is not named in the Book of Esther, but his slimy, evil presence is felt. Spiritual warfare is being unleashed in heavenly places. The power that would destroy continues to war against the power that would deliver.

The king has sentenced a large part of the population to a certain death. He does not realize it yet, but his edict will reach into the royal palace and affect his queen. While the couriers are out delivering this deadly decree, what does the king do? Esther 3:15 says, *The king and Haman sat down to drink (while)the city of Susa was in confusion.* The king and Haman decreed the annihilation of the Jews and then sat down to eat and drink. Just how hardened does a heart have to be to declare a national ethnic cleansing and then sit down and eat? The stage is set for God to act!

God is in covenant with Israel. From the conception of this fledgling nation Satan has declared war against God's chosen people. Haman's name can be included with those of Pharaoh, Herod, and Hitler as a few of the ungodly men Satan has used to threaten God's chosen people with annihilation. In Genesis 12:3 God tells Abraham, "*And I will bless those who bless you, and the one who curses you I will curse.*" God says to Israel, "*No weapon that is formed against you will prosper*" (Isa. 54:17). God's hand is on His chosen people.

Satan's wicked schemes to interrupt the lineage of Christ have always been overridden by God's sovereign power. In Herod's day Satan attempts to wipe out the life of the babe of Bethlehem. When Satan's plan is thwarted, he begins to plot to do away with Jesus by crucifixion. Surely Jesus' demise will paralyze His followers with fear and put a stop to the spread of the gospel. Satan undoubtedly thinks he has won when the body of Jesus lies lifeless in the tomb. Satan gloats with joy and celebrates his hard-fought victory. Demons dance. Satan sings. Hell has a holiday. But wait . . . what happens?

The Lord is raised from the dead! The tomb is empty, victory is won, and evil will not triumph! Paul writes, *O death, where is your victory? O death, where is your sting? The sting of death is sin, and the power of sin is the law; but thanks be to God, who gives us the victory through our Lord Jesus Christ* (1 Cor. 15:55-57).

A queen understands that the cross of Jesus Christ has defeated her enemy. She also acknowledges the enemy retains limited power until the end of the age. At that time Jesus will cast him into the lake of fire. In Revelation 12:12 John writes, *Woe to the earth and the sea, because the devil has come down to you, having great wrath, knowing that he has only a short time.* Until that time, a queen arms herself spiritually, guards herself mentally and stays on the alert. All the way, she goes about her kingdom doing good. Being a queen is a fulltime job!

A Dramatic Display

Read Esther 4:1-17

The news went out impelled by the king's command while the decree was issued at the citadel in Susa (Esth. 3:15). Wicked Haman tricks the king into giving his stamp of approval to a police action that will exterminate as many as 15 million Jewish people. The cold reality of the Jews' impending annihilation shakes them to the very core of their beings. Do we have any reason to wonder that *the city of Susa was in confusion* (Esth. 3:15)?

Panic seizes the hearts of the Jewish people as the ramifications of the edict strike them like a blow to the midsection. They already are living in exile as the trophies of war. Now they are faced with total obliteration!

**1. Read Esther 4:1-2. What is Mordecai's response to the frightening news?

_____

Mordecai reacts with great emotion. He *wailed loudly and bitterly* (Esth. 4:1). He feels responsible for bringing the entire Jewish nation into jeopardy. Haman's reaction to Mordecai's offense is out of proportion. It merely has given Haman an excuse to vent his anti-Semitic views.

Sick with grief, Mordecai tears his clothes and puts on sackcloth and ashes. In Esther's day the practice of rending garments and wearing sackcloth and ashes was a common expression of guilt. Mourners often dressed in sackcloth as an expression of the depth of their pain and grief. These typically were coarse, loose-fitting garments made of goat's hair. Often those who were grief-stricken would take ashes from the remains of a fire, throw them in the air, and allow the ash to drift down on them. The billowing ash gave them a ghastly and unclean appearance as a vivid expression of their anguish. While our modern-day society usually grieves in rather subdued ways, the Eastern culture still deals with grief with much weeping and wailing and other dramatic displays of sorrow and sadness.

Mordecai is despondent with grief for himself, his people, and for his beloved cousin. *He went as far as the king's gate, for no one was to enter the king's gate clothed in sackcloth* (Esth. 4:2). Mordecai knows he will not be able to have an encounter with the king. Evidently Esther, during her reign, has been separated from direct contact with Mordecai. Perhaps he goes to the king's gate in hopes of capturing the attention of the queen. She is probably unaware of the edict. Her role in the monarchy keeps her in a secluded, protected environment in the harem. He knows the thick stone walls of the palace will not be able to protect Esther from the deadly edict of the king. Mordecai's pain knows no bounds.

Beloved mom, learn this about sorrow and pain. God does not waste suffering. When He allows His child to go through a painful experience, He supplies the grace to walk though the difficult circumstances. He uses it to bring glory to Himself. The lost world is confounded when it watches a Christian walk unscathed through the fiery furnace. God gets the glory when the suffering refines His children and produces in them the image of Christ.

God is in the perfecting business with His people. While He accepts us just as we are when we accept Him, He loves us too much to leave us in that condition. From the moment of conversion He designs circumstances that will challenge our faith and strengthen our resolve to walk with Him.

**2. Read James 1:2-4. What is the proper Christian response to the trials of life?

_____

Why?

_____

What is end result of endurance?

_____

Write about a time God tested your faith. What did you learn from the experience?

_____

_____

_____

Suffering is not pleasant, but suffering is profitable in the life of a committed Christian. In Romans 8:18 Paul says, *For I consider that the sufferings of this present time are not worthy to be compared with the glory that is to be revealed to us.* While no one wants to experience pain, God knows how to mete out our affliction in doses that we can tolerate to train us to walk by faith. In 2 Corinthians 4:17 Paul writes, *For momentary light affliction is producing for us an eternal weight of glory far beyond all comparison.* Suffering, rightly understood, produces sanctification in this life and eternal reward in the next.

3. Suffering builds Christian character if we yield to the skillful, albeit painful, touch of the Refiner's fire. Read 2 Corinthians 1:3-7. According to this passage, what is one of God's purposes in suffering?

_____

What can we learn from the experience?

How does our suffering benefit others?

Sorrow and suffering are part of the price of living in a sin-sick world. While we cannot always understand the mysterious ways of God, we can rest in His sovereign purpose and plan for our lives. We can trust His heart even when we cannot clearly see His face in the midst of difficult trials.

A season of suffering is painful at best. Psalm 30:5 says, *Weeping may last for the night, but a shout of joy comes in the morning.* The psalmist goes on to say, *You have turned for me my mourning into dancing; You have loosed my sackcloth, and girded me with gladness, that my soul may sing praise to Thee, and not be silent. O Lord my God, I will give thanks to Thee forever* (Ps. 30:11-12). The end-product of suffering is the sound of joy bells in the heart. It produces a depth of gratitude and praise that cannot have been fathomed apart from the dark night of the soul. *It is good for me that I was afflicted, that I may learn Your statutes* (Ps. 119:71).

Mordecai is heartsick when he hears of the king's decree. In his agony of soul he seeks the face of the Lord and cries out with utterances that can not be articulated. Although the dark clouds of suffering try to obscure the face of God, He still is in control. He remains on the throne! Hallelujah! What a Savior!

The faith-walk forces a queen to look beyond the temporal to the eternal. Regardless of circumstances a queen looks to Jesus and experiences soul rest even as storm clouds gather.

A Passionate Plea

Read Esther 4:1-17

With a penstroke the Jewish population is placed under a death sentence. The impact of the deadly decree spreads across the kingdom and leaves a swath of agony and grief in its wake. A condemned people unashamedly engage in public displays of agony and grief. *Many lay on sackcloth and ashes* (Esth. 4:3). A great dragnet of evil soon will spread across the kingdom. Its web of hatred and prejudice will ensnare the Jewish population.

Here is a people under the sentence of death. Helpless and hopeless, these people are in desperate need of rescue. Their lineage places them in the line of Abraham. All his descendants are condemned to die because of a writ against them. This is an apt description of anyone outside of a personal relationship with Jesus Christ.

Profound parallels can be drawn from the story of Esther. We too are born under a sentence of death. In Ephesians 2:12 Paul writes, *Remember that you were at that time separate from Christ, excluded from the commonwealth of Israel, and strangers to the covenants of promise, having no hope and without God in the world.* We were born in bondage to the curse of sin. We were hopeless and helpless and in need of a Savior. Romans 5:12 says, *Therefore, just as through one man sin entered into the world, and death through sin, and so death spread to all men, because all sinned.* Our lineage placed us in Adam and in Adam all die (1 Cor. 15:22). According to Romans 6:12, sin reigns in our mortal bodies; therefore, we become enemies of God. Paul says we were dead in our transgressions and sins *in which (we) formerly walked according to the course of this world, according to the prince of the power of the air, of the spirit that is now working in the sons of disobedience* (Eph. 2:1-2). We were *indulging the desires of the flesh and of the mind, and were by nature children of wrath* (Eph. 2:3). A writ of condemnation is held against us. We are held captive by sin, self, and Satan. We are destined to die and go to hell. Like the Jews of Esther's day, we desperately need a Savior who can rescue us, ransom us, and redeem us from the power of sin, death, and the grave. With Paul we cry out, *"Wretched man that I am! Who will set me free from the body of this death?"* (Rom. 7:24).

The only answer to the age-old question of sin is the shed blood of the Lord Jesus Christ. In Romans 7:25a Paul writes, *Thanks be to God through Jesus Christ our Lord!* Colossians 2:13-14 says, *And when you were dead in your transgressions and the uncircumcision of your flesh, He made you alive together with Him, having forgiven us all our transgressions, having canceled out the certificate of debt consisting of decrees against us and which was hostile to us; and He has taken it out of the way, having nailed it to the cross.* Hallelujah! What a Savior! Christ is God's remedy for man's ruin.

In the Garden of Eden Adam gives away the estate of humankind to Satan. Adam's disobedience plunges his descendants into damnable sin. Since the estate is lost by a person, a person will be required to retrieve it. However, this cannot be any human being. Deity clothed in humanity is required to redeem and reconcile sinful humanity to a holy God. Romans 5:19 says, *For as through the one man's disobedience the many were made sinners, even so through the obedience of the One the many will be made righteous.* In Adam we became sinners; in Christ we become saints!

The Jews' response to the deadly decree is accompanied by weeping and wailing over the wretchedness of their situation. The Jews recognize how hopeless things are; they grieve and agonize. Sadly, such raw emotion over the consequences of sin is missing in our culture and even in our churches today. Conspicuously absent is conviction about sin. Mordecai understands the seriousness of the king's deadly decree. He tears his clothes, puts on sackcloth with ashes, and publicly demonstrates the anguish of his soul. The swirling winds of evil threaten to destroy him and his people. In the center of the city, Mordecai with a loud and bitter cry weeps bitter tears and laments his loss with a loud and bitter cry. Jews all over the kingdom mourn, fast, and weep.

**1. Read Esther 4:4. When Queen Esther learns of Mordecai's anguish, what does she do?

_____

What is his response?

_____

We can only imagine Esther's anguish of soul when she discovers Mordecai in sackcloth and ashes. She can not speak to him directly. She most likely has no idea what has transpired. In an attempt to comfort him Esther sends out a change of clothes. Mordecai refuses the garments. More than a new wardrobe will be needed to avert this crisis.

Don't miss the application. Many people attempt to deal with the sin issue by putting on the garment of religious respectability. The covering of religious ritual will not remove the fact that we are guilty sinners before a holy God. Nor will religious activity alter the fact that the wages of sin is death. No amount of external religion or rule-keeping can wash away our sins. Nothing but the blood of Jesus can pay our sin debt! Isaiah 1:18 says, *"Come now, and let us reason together,"* says the Lord, *"Though your sins are as scarlet, they will be as white as snow; though they are red like crimson, they will be like wool."*

Salvation is only through the shed blood of Jesus Christ. Acts 4:12 says, *And there is salvation in no one else; for there is no other name under heaven that has been given among men, by which we must be saved.*

**2. Read John 3:1-7. What does Jesus tell Nicodemus about salvation?

Romans 3:23 says, *For all have sinned and fall short of the glory of God.* Romans 6:23 says, *The wages of sin is death.* Everyone is born a sinner in need of a Savior. Romans 5:8 says, *But God demonstrates His own love toward us, in that while we were yet sinners, Christ died for us.* Through the shed blood of the Lord Jesus Christ, God makes a way of escape. The Bible says Jesus died for the sins of the whole world. John writes, *And He Himself is the propitiation for our sins; and not for ours only, but also for those of the whole world* (1 John 2:2). However, His blood is only applied to the sin debt of those who receive Him by faith. Personally invite Christ into your life to forgive your sins and take you to heaven when you die. Romans 10:9-10 says, *If you confess with your mouth Jesus as Lord, and believe in your heart that God raised Him from the dead, you shall be saved; for with the heart a person believes, resulting in righteousness, and with the mouth he confesses, resulting in salvation.* Salvation is in Jesus Christ. It is a free gift to all who believe. Romans 10:13 says, *Whoever will call upon the name of the Lord will be saved.*

Mordecai knows that the situation facing the Jews calls for much more than a change of clothes. He recognizes the severity of the situation and the dire need for God to bring forth a deliverer. In the same way, recognize your own human depravity. Cry out to the only One who can deliver you from the bondage of sin.

What can wash away my sin? Nothing but the blood of Jesus Christ!

A Divine Appointment

Read Esther 4:1-17

Esther sends Hathach to the city square to speak to Mordecai. *Mordecai told him all that had happened to him and the exact amount of money that Haman has promised to pay to the king's treasuries for the destruction of the Jews. He also gives him a copy of the text of the edict which has been issued in Susa for their destruction, that he might show Esther and inform her, and to order her to go in to the king to implore his favor and to plead with him for her people. Hathach came back and related Mordecai's words to Esther* (Esth. 4:8-9).

Once again Esther is placed in an impossible situation. According to the law of the Medes and Persians anyone who approaches the king without being summoned will be promptly put to death unless the king extends his golden scepter. If Esther appears before the king without an invitation, she can possibly lose her life. If she does not venture an appeal to the king, the Jewish people will lose their lives. Either way she faces a certain death.

Esther sends word to Mordecai and reminds him of the royal protocol. Mordecai knows his request is serious. The fact he has not been allowed to speak to her for five years has not hardened his heart to her plight. She is like a daughter to him. His plans for her life are irretrievably changed when the king's men seize her, force her from her cousin's home, and place her in the king's harem. Now she stands on the threshold of another terrible event.

Mordecai tells Hathach and the others to take his reply to Esther. Mordecai says, *"Do not imagine that you in the king's palace can escape any more than all the Jews"* (Esth. 4:13). Remember Mordecai has advised Esther to keep her nationality secret. All the years she has been sequestered in the palace, she appears to have honored the request. Now the time is right for Esther to identify with her people. Mordecai has this in mind when he says, *"For if you remain silent at this time, relief and deliverance will arise for the Jews from another place and you and your father's house will perish"* (Esth. 4:14).

Although Mordecai implores Esther to make an appeal to stop the mindless slaughter of the Jewish people, he does not want her to feel indispensable. God's will does not depend on the success of a person or persons. He is not limited by the frailties and failures of His people.

He is able to supersede any situation. Mordecai knows God will always preserve a Jewish remnant, just as He promises Abraham. If Esther does not step up and do what she can to protect the line of Christ by defending the Jews, God will surely rise up another in her place.

**1. Read Romans 11:2-4. Elijah begins to believe that he is indispensable and that somehow the success of God's work relies on him alone. What does Elijah say?

_____

What is God's response to the prophet?

_____

Elijah is not indispensable; God has 7,000 men prepared to continue His work. God is never at the mercy of human effort. His will is not derailed by His people's inabilities. God always has a plan; He will prevail, even if He has to circumvent us to accomplish it. Esther has a divine appointment, but she is not indispensable. If she is not willing, God will raise up another.

I boarded a plane in Knoxville, TN, and prepared for the flight home. I had just spoken to a wonderful women's group. I was physically, mentally, emotionally, and spiritually exhausted. My overwhelming fatigue was directly related to a severe sinus infection that I battled. Steeled with antibiotics, I had not traveled well. The infection settled in my ears and was making flying very uncomfortable. Desperate to get home, I fell into my assigned seat and buckled my seat belt. I closed my eyes and prayed for the pain in my head and ears to ease enough to tolerate the short flight. I intended to spend the trip dozing—lost in the drone of the aircraft's engines and the hum of the unintelligible chatter of other passengers around me. As my unidentified seatmate slid in next to me, I barely opened my eyes to acknowledge her presence as I slipped back into the realm of antihistamine-induced fog.

"Aren't you Jean Stockdale?" my traveling companion asked enthusiastically. "You are just the person I need to talk to," she declared with delight. As the haze in my numbed brain parted, I knew that I had arrived at a divine appointment. Sleep would have to be postponed for my assignment. I trusted God to clear my head and give me the power and grace to overcome my headache and become engaged in this young woman's needs.

As moms, we tend to live rather routine, ordinary lives. Our days are consumed with tending little ones, doing laundry, paying bills, cooking meals, cleaning house, making beds, picking up toys, doing yard work, going grocery shopping, and running endless errands. Days turn into weeks; weeks quietly drift into months of monotony, as they are punctuated occasionally with a crisis or two. Generally speaking our lives are rather mundane and commonplace. If you believe that, you do not understand God's purpose and plan for your life! If you know the Lord Jesus Christ, He has set you on the path of a marvelous adventure. Every day with Jesus is wrought with opportunities, prospects, miracles, and divine appointments.

Divine appointments are a natural part of the Christian life. Sadly, our spiritual antennas are bent; we miss God's ordained engagements. We are guilty of glibly going about our busy days without giving a thought to His agenda. Look to the Lord and ask Him to illuminate your spiritual eyes of understanding. Ask Him to help you to see Him at work. Psalm 119:130 says, *The unfolding of Your words gives light; it gives understanding to the simple.* God's Word is our external control. God's indwelling Holy Spirit is our internal control.

Failing to spend time in the Word of God or disobeying the Spirit of God surely leads to disaster in our Christian experience. Saturate your soul with the Word. Walk in His ways. Psalm 119:147-148 says, *I rise before dawn and cry for help; I wait for Your words. My eyes anticipate the night watches, that I may meditate on Your word.* Treasure the Word of God. Meditate on it. Memorize it. Love it.

**2. Read James 1:22-25. According to this passage what is necessary to become a faithful follower of Jesus Christ?

_____

Practically speaking, how can you become a doer of the Word and not merely a hearer?

_____

The secret to supernatural living is to look intently at the perfect law and abide by it. A quick glance into the Word of God in a Sunday sermon or a casual glimpse into God's Holy Scriptures during the week will not be sufficient. A cavalier approach to the Word will not arm you against the onslaught of the evil one or give you spiritual sensitivity to the subtle moves of God. In 1 Corinthians 4:2 Paul says, *It is required of stewards that one be found trustworthy.* If you intend to walk in communion with the Father and be used for His kingdom work, *be diligent to present yourself approved to God as a workman who does not need to be ashamed, accurately handling the word of truth* (2 Tim. 2:15). Mordecai understands the spiritual reality of divine appointments. Esther has a divine appointment. If she fails to rise to the occasion, God will raise up another.

Learn this, beloved mom, about God's purposes. God's will is never thwarted by human failure. He does not depend on His human creation's ability to perform. God is never at a loss because we fail to carry out His will. He will find another whose heart is turned toward Him. Second Chronicles 16:9 says, *For the eyes of the Lord move to and fro throughout the earth that He may strongly support those whose heart is completely His.* God is not held hostage by our inability to follow His directions or our insensitivity to His Spirit. He will simply seek out another to do His bidding. How sad to miss God's plan for your life because of carnality or immaturity!

Esther faces a defining moment—a crossroads where conviction and courage merge. *Mordecai said, "And who knows whether you have not attained royalty for such a time as this?"* (Esth. 4:14). God has ordained her circumstances. He has placed her in a time and place in which He can use her to deliver His people from certain death. She has a divine appointment. The only question remaining is whether she will obey or shy away from her calling.

A queen keeps a royal schedule, but she develops sensitivity to the stirring of the Holy Spirit. She allows for divine appointments. As a member of the monarchy she is prepared to fulfill her royal calling, regardless of the cost. She represents her King well

Weekly Summary

Please record insights gleaned from this week's study.

_____
_____
_____
_____
_____
_____
_____
_____
_____
_____
_____
_____
_____
_____
_____
_____
_____
_____
_____
_____
_____
_____

A Determined Declaration

Read Esther 4:1-17

Esther is standing face-to-face with her destiny. In this defining moment her strength of character will be revealed. Theology and reality will meet. Courage and convictions will merge.

When confronted with an excruciatingly difficult decision, Esther makes a determined declaration. With eyes shining, cheeks glowing, and absolute resolve ringing in her voice, Esther doggedly declares, *"I will go in to the king, which is not according to the law"* (Esth. 4:16c). For 30 days the king has not summoned her. Now she is prepared to breach royal protocol and stand in the gap for her people. Who knows how the Gentile king will respond to her Jewish heritage? How will he receive her appeal? Esther casts herself on the grace of God and rests in His divine providence as she proclaims, *"If I perish, I perish"* (Esth. 4:16d).

Circumstances will break in on our lives and expose our level of spiritual maturity. Sadly, many Christians glibly toss around the correct spiritual jargon without possessing genuine spiritual power. God uses crisises to test our hearts and reveal our strength of character. This exercise is not to show God what lurks in the recesses of the heart. God already knows the truth about the measure of spiritual reality in each of His children. He knows that we must be forced to see the results. Otherwise, our own flesh can deceive us and cause us to presume we are more spiritual than we are. The crisis moments of our lives spontaneously reveal the authenticity of our spiritual growth and maturity. Sadly, we often are found lacking.

The Christian life is a series of challenges that God uses to train us to walk by faith and not sight. We rely on our five senses. We operate in a realm of logic. Biblical faith runs contrary to every natural human response. That is why God must be an integral part of the equation!

**1. Esther's faith is put to the test and she came forth as pure gold, as Job 23:10 says. Read 1 Peter 1:6-8. According to this test what is the true value of trials and tribulations?

_____

What is the end result of the testing of our faith?

_____

Most of us believe careful planning will allow us to determine the course of our lives. While God instructs us to be wise, the life of faith continually casts itself on the sovereignty of God. God is at work. He is mysteriously and silently working through a series of seemingly coincidental events and human decisions. He even is able to use those based on evil intent to perform His purposes and plans. The eye of faith is necessary to see His handprint, but He is at work.

Some years ago I unexpectedly began to experience blurred vision. Although I have worn glasses or contacts since I was a child, I never had experienced any difficulty with my eyes. I was becoming increasingly alarmed. *Maybe I am going blind*, I thought. *Perhaps this is the precursor to losing my sight.* As a Bible teacher, I rely heavily on my ability to see clearly. I was threatened by the prospect of having a problem with my vision. Arriving at my ophthalmologist's office I found myself gripped with anxiety and dread. I feared his impending diagnosis. As my physician began the examination, in great detail I described the difficulty I was experiencing and then braced myself for his verdict. As he began his explanation, I took a deep breath and attempted to slow my rapid shallow breathing, lower my escalating blood pressure, and calm my pounding heart. "Lord," I silently prayed. "Give me the strength to endure this difficult diagnosis. Amen."

"Well, as I see it," my doctor began, "the only problem is that your contacts are in serious need of professional cleaning."

"That's all," I squeaked as my words caught in my throat. "My contacts are dirty. That is all that is wrong with my eyes. I have dirty contacts. I thought I was going blind!" My doctor, amused at my pathetic attempt at self-diagnosis, laughed along with me as I slumped back against the chair in gales of relieved laughter.

Most of us do not know how to see clearly with the eyes of faith. Our failure to study the Word of God causes us to view the world through lenses blurred with the corruption of this world. Consequently, we often are unaware of God's work in our lives. We are so spiritually dull, we fail to recognize the quiet stirring of God in our lives.

Esther is the queen, yet she is bound by the ironclad laws of Persian court etiquette. Evidently, Haman has unrestricted access to the king; Esther does not. Esther finds herself caught between the Gentile world of the pagan court and the Jewish world in which she has been reared. *For such a time as this*, Esther has been placed in the palace. With no regard for her personal safety, she prepares to identify with God's covenant people.

As Esther readies herself to stand before the king and plead for her people, she instructs Mordecai to gather the Jews and proclaim a three-day fast. She and her maidens will also participate. Esther's request implies that she is regularly spending time in prayer and communion with the Lord. Although God's name is not mentioned in the Book of Esther, His presence is very much apparent.

In the Bible, resurrection often is associated with the number three. In the mind of the child of God three days of fasting instantly evokes the death, burial, and resurrection of Christ. Esther needs the power of God on her life. She seeks it with prayer and fasting. What is being required of her will require death to self. The fast represents this.

Fasting is a physical discipline that produces spiritual results. Time usually spent in meal preparation and eating is dedicated to the Lord. Every hunger pang brings to mind the urgent prayer needs. Fasting, a discipline often ignored by Christians, allows for protracted periods of prayer and quiet reflection on the things of God. Refusing to coddle the physical body allows the believer to die to self and develop a fresh perspective on being alive to Christ.

Esther knows she needs supernatural strength. She asks others to pray. This is a spiritual principle we do not want to overlook. Conversion places us not only in the body of Christ but in the family of God. We are in a spiritual community. We are living stones *being built up as a spiritual house for a holy priesthood, to offer up spiritual sacrifices acceptable to God through Jesus Christ* (1 Pet. 2:5). We are commanded to *pray for one another* (Jam. 5:16). Esther rallies her people to fast and pray.

A queen knows how to pray. Although she is in an exalted position, she is a woman under authority. She knows how to make her requests known to God. She seeks Him daily in prayer. In times of great difficulty she adds the spiritual discipline of fasting. A queen knows how to stand and strike a regal pose. Moreover, a queen knows how to kneel.

Esther knows deliverance is from God. Psalm 75:6-7 says, *For not from the east, nor from the west, nor from the desert comes exaltation; but God is the Judge; He puts down one and exalts another.* Esther casts herself on the mercy of God and rests in His providential care. May God grant us a heart like Esther has so we can face the testing of our faith and triumphantly respond, *"If I perish, I perish."*

A Courageous Queen

Read Esther 5: 1-14

Esther and the Jews face a dilemma of epic proportions. They need God to stand strong on their behalf. Beseeching Him with prayer and fasting demonstrates their sincere desire to have their petitions heard by the Father and answered accordingly. Esther, through prayer and fasting, devotes this time without the distractions of food to wait on the Lord and allow Him to guide her thoughts and help her frame her words.

**1. Esther needs supernatural power. She knows how to appropriate it through prayer and supplication. Read Isaiah 40:31. What is God's remedy for exhausted Christians who need strength and endurance?

_____

As a young mom with two little ones under the age of 3, I was totally exhausted. A stupor, brought on by lack of sleep, made my daily routine difficult and regularly sent me spiraling downward into a state of despair. Frazzled and fatigued, I was highly volatile and very emotional. Tears occurred easily without explanation or warning. I was overwhelmed and over-tired. Like all who share the sisterhood of motherhood, I was suffering from the lack of a hot meal, a hot shower, and a moment to myself.

After one especially difficult night of trying to get two little boys to sleep, in a sleep-deprived fog I shuffled into the kitchen. On my refrigerator my husband had handwritten Isaiah 40:31 and taped it at eye level. It read, *Those who wait for the Lord will gain new strength; they will mount up with wings like eagles, they will run and not get tired, they will walk and not become weary.* For months I read it every morning and tried to remind myself to lean on the Lord. His supernatural strength is required for all Christians, especially mothers.

Esther is desperate. The Jews have the sentence of death looming over them. She bombards the gates of heaven with prayer and fasting on behalf of herself and her people. Prayer is an effective means of communication with our Heavenly Father. Prayer combined with fasting is especially powerful.

2. This truth is illustrated in Matthew 17:14-21. Read this text. What spiritual conclusion can you draw from this passage?

Some situations are so demanding we may want to consider adding the spiritual discipline of fasting to enhance our prayer lives. Because of Esther's interlude of concentrated prayer and fasting, she can enter the king's presence with courage and confidence.

**3.God is sovereignly in control, although from our limited human perspective this does not always appear to be so. Look up Psalm 118:23. What does this verse teach us about God's ability to orchestrate circumstances to accomplish His divine purposes?

Memorize this verse. Learn this truth. This is a spiritual principle that I have prayed and claimed many times in my life when I have faced obstacles that were out of my control and decisions that were out of my hands. I can gladly testify that God has always been true to Himself. He works in the hearts and lives of those in positions of authority to bring about His will. I have learned to rest in the Lord and trust in His timing to do what is best for my family and me. Trust in the Lord. He knows what He is about in our lives.

Esther, confident of God's direction and assured of His presence and power, approaches the throne. *Now it came about on the third day that Esther put on her royal robes and stood in the inner court of the king's palace in front of the king's rooms, and the king was sitting on his royal throne in the throne room, opposite the entrance to the palace* (Esth. 5:1). Wearing her royal robes Esther approaches the king. Her decision to appear in her regalia tells us she is claiming her authority and power as the queen. As Christians we are clothed in the right-eousness of Christ. Paul writes, *He made Him who knew no sin to be sin on our behalf, so that we might become the righteousness of God in Him* (2 Cor. 5:21). *For all of you who were baptized into Christ have clothed yourselves with Christ* (Gal. 3:27). Clothed in his right-eousness, we stand in the power and authority of Jesus Christ.

Esther 5:2 says, *And it happened when the king saw Esther the queen standing in the court, she obtained favor in his sight; and the king extended to Esther the golden scepter which was in his hand.* The king extends grace to Esther, who desperately needs it. Without it, she will surely be put to death with no explanation and no opportunity to plead her case or intercede for her people.

Noticing Esther's distraught expression, the king asks the nature of her concern. Instead of blurting out her dilemma in a tumble of emotions and tears, Esther demonstrates strength under control. Again we would be wise to learn this spiritual principle. When we wait on the Lord, we learn the release of the Holy Sprit as well as the restraint of the Holy Spirit. He directs our words and prevents us from responding inappropriately.

Esther invites the king and Haman to a banquet she has been preparing. Let me hasten to remind you that Esther has been fasting for the last three days while she is preparing a sumptuous meal fit for a king. Again we see the strength of her character and the enormous control Esther exercises. Although fasting is a spiritual exercise, it does not negate the hunger pains. In fact, it seems to intensify them!

Esther has declared a three-day fast; she intends to be true to her vow. Ecclesiastes 5:5 says, *It is better that you should not vow than that you should vow and not pay.* As Christians we are compelled to walk in integrity. We say what we mean and mean what we say. In Matthew 5:37 Jesus said, *"But let your statement be, 'Yes, yes' or 'No, no'; anything beyond these is of evil."* Esther is a woman of her word.

The king quickly accepts Esther's offer for a banquet. Haman is summoned. As they linger over the meal, the king once again questions Esther about her matter of concern. Esther has breached royal protocol by approaching the king without an invitation. Surely something quite serious is troubling her—something she is willing to risk her reign and her life to make known to the king. As the king presses her for details, Esther says, *"If I have found favor in the sight of the king, and if it please the king to grant my petition and do what I request, may the king and Haman come to the banquet which I shall prepare for them, and tomorrow I will do as the king says"* (Esth. 5:8).

Esther wisely understands the value of timing. She is not in a hurry. She is not looking for revenge or retribution. Esther is walking by faith. She is resting in God's sovereign purpose and plan. Had God not involved Himself in the events of her life, Esther would have been dead rather than dining with the king!

Clearly, the king is oblivious to God's involvement in the events as they unfold. He considers himself invincible. He is the king of most of the known world. Little does he know God is working behind the scenes. God is invisible, but He is always busy. He is moving in a multitude of places and orchestrating circumstances that are beyond our control. The king may have ruled the kingdom of Persia, but the Lord is in control of His universe. Haman may have attempted to seal the fate of a nation with the stroke of his pen, but God remains in charge. In Isaiah 66:1 the Lord says, *"Heaven is My throne, and the earth is My footstool."* He has providentially placed Esther at the epicenter of His divine plan.

Just as God places Esther in the palace *for such a time as this*, He has divinely appointed you to serve Him as a wife and a mom. Mothering may not seem as glamorous as being ensconced in the royal palace draped in diamonds and swathed in silk with servants at your beck and call, but fulfilling God's call on your life is the place of true satisfaction and joy. Colossians 3:23-24 says, *Whatever you do, do your work heartily as for the Lord rather than for men, knowing that from the Lord you will receive the reward of the inheritance. It is the Lord Christ whom you serve.* Whether you are in a castle or a condo, live like a queen and serve the Lord with a cheerful heart. Know that He has a purpose and a plan for your life.

A Pompous Prime Minister

Read Esther 5:1-14

If ever pride were personified in a human being, Haman is that man. The psalmist describes the wicked as being filled with audacity and arrogance. This is an apt description of our man, Haman. Psalm 73:6-9 says, *Therefore pride is their necklace; the garment of violence covers them. Their eye bulges from fatness; the imaginations of their heart run riot. They mock, and wickedly speak of oppression; they speak from on high. They have set their mouth against the heavens, and their tongue parades through the earth.* The writer of this psalm could not have more aptly described the narcissistic Haman. He has an inflated sense of self and a haughty air of superiority. Be careful, Haman. The Bible says, *Therefore let him who thinks he stands take heed that he does not fall* (1 Cor. 10:12).

Haman was invited to a private banquet as the one and only guest of the king and queen of Persia. Now he has been invited back for another private audience with the royal family. Haman is intoxicated with the power and privilege that has been extended to him. Esther 5:9 says, *Then Haman went out that day glad and pleased of heart.* His ego cannot be contained. Haman is strutting about the palace like a peacock. He brags about his self-importance and flaunts his inflated ego.

**1. Proverbs has much to say about the danger of pride. Look up the following verses and write down your insights.

a. Proverbs 6:16-17

_____

b. Proverbs 16:5

_____

c. Proverbs 18:12

_____

d. Proverbs 21:4

_____

e. Proverbs 29:23

_____

As children of God we have no room for pride. We are the happy recipients of grace. As such, we cannot take credit for anything good in our lives. Jesus in us, the hope of glory, makes us who we are. Paul writes, _For if anyone thinks he is something when he is nothing, he deceives himself_ (Gal. 6:3). We have nothing to boast about except Jesus. _But may it never be that I would boast, except in the cross of our Lord Jesus Christ, through which the world has been crucified to me, and I to the world_ (Gal. 6:14). We are basking in the glory of God's grace toward us. As humble servants of the Lord, guard against the subtle and insidious sway of pride. In 1 Corinthians 4:7 Paul writes, _And what do you have that you did not receive? But if you did receive it, why do you boast as if you had not received it._ Let us learn to live with a humble heart, grateful for the gift of grace. James 4:6 says, _God is opposed to the proud, but gives grace to the humble._ Grace. Grace. Marvelous grace! Thank God for His amazing grace!

Haman is drunk with pride. Nothing can spoil his good mood. Nothing that is, until he sees Mordecai in the king's gate. _He did not stand up or tremble before him_ (Esth. 5:9). Mordecai has been a continual thorn in the side of Haman. For weeks his insolence and indifference toward Haman's authority has been festering. _Haman was filled with anger against Mordecai_ (Esth. 5:9).

To ease his seething anger, Haman gathers his family and friends. For his captive audience he begins an endless recital of his achievements. Haman is consumed with his own adulation. He recounts _every instance where the king has magnified him, and how he had promoted him above the princes and servants of the king_ (Esth. 5:11). That is, Haman hosts a party to narrate his accomplishments. That must have been a great party!

The crowd advises Haman to take action against Mordecai, the bane of his existence. _They said, "Have a gallows fifty cubits high made and in the morning ask the king to have Mordecai hanged on it, then go joyfully with the king to the banquet"_ (Esth. 5:14). Haman loves the idea. Kill Mordecai and then go stuff himself at a banquet. A villain like Haman loves such a plan! Just reading it gives me indigestion, but it wouldn't have that effect on Haman. The combination of death and dining makes his mouth salivate.

The Persians did not hang their victims with a rope. The Persians' method of execution was to impale the condemned on a stake and hoist them into the air to die a humiliating and tortuous death. In this case the stake is 75 feet high. Envisioning Mordecai being run through with an enormous stake and hoisted into the air as a monument to his authority pleases Haman immensely. That will teach him! No one will ever defy Haman again and live to tell about it!

Driven by murder and madness, Haman that night is lulled to sleep as he listens to the hammering of the construction crew. Through the night the crew works to prepare the gallows. Perhaps he dreams of Mordecai's horrendous and agonizing death and longs to savor the sweet taste of vengeance.

To the casual observer, God may not appear to be in control of this situation. Evil appears to triumph over good. The situation may seem impossible. Beloved, that is when God does His best work! Psalm 61:2-4 says, *From the end of the earth I call to You, when my heart is faint; lead me to the rock that is higher than I. For You have been a refuge for me, a tower of strength against the enemy. Let me dwell in Your tent forever; let me take refuge in the shelter of Your wings.*

Beloved mom, fix your eyes on the lovely face of Jesus; trust in Him. Psalm 91:1 says, *He who dwells in the shelter of the Most High will abide in the shadow of the Almighty.* A queen knows where to stand. Stand in the shelter of the Most High. Abide in His shadow.

A Disregarded Deed

Read Esther 6:1-14

On Tuesday, July 22, 2003, Memphis, TN, was struggling to recover from one of the worst storms in the Mid-South's history. Straight-line winds, clocked at nearly 100 miles an hour, blew through the Memphis area. The violent storm left massive, uprooted trees and severe property damage in its wake. Immediately after the storm more than 300,000 homes and businesses were without power. At least four deaths were directly attributed to the ferocious storm. Debris, along with broken limbs and fallen trees, littered the streets. Because of the massive power outage, finding a restaurant or even a fast-food vendor up and running was difficult. Memphians began to frantically scramble in an effort to survive in a situation that was rapidly deteriorating. No power. No lights. No air-conditioning. No food. No way!

A friend of mine managed to find a hamburger stand open with a long line of hungry and hot patrons waiting somewhat patiently. Three men in line behind her were commiserating about the miserable living conditions brought on by the storm. Each man shared his harrowing tales of chaos and cleanup in the aftermath of the violent storm. These men were stunned when another man in line relayed his story. Earlier that day, he had driven through a neighborhood clogged with fallen trees and limbs. As he carefully picked his way through the jumbled street, he saw several good Samaritans using chain saws to clear the debris. His path was blocked by a large limb that one of the men was diligently cutting up to remove. The driver got out of his vehicle and left the door open and the engine running while he went to help the man drag the large limb to the curb. In that brief interlude, another man ran toward the men as if to help. Instead, he jumped into the idling vehicle and sped away! Just when you think things cannot get worse, they usually do!

What is true about life today is certainly true in Esther's day in our Bible story. All of the Jews are sentenced to die in a matter of months. Now Mordecai is about to be impaled on a stake and hung in the air to die a cruel and torturous death.

Beloved moms, when the night seasons of life arrive, *fix your eyes on Jesus* (Heb. 12:1-2) and do not be dismayed. A queen knows the importance of eye-contact with the King. A heavenly glimpse of His lovely face will ease your pain and calm your fears. Learn to live in the presence of the Lord Jesus Christ.

At this point the story of Esther takes quite an unexpected turn. Haman has arranged for the extermination of all the Jews and the execution of Mordecai. On the surface things look very bleak for our heroes, but God is silently and providentially moving.

Think back in the story of Esther and Mordecai. Mordecai bravely exposes a conspiracy against the king after he overhears two men scheming to murder the monarch. Mordecai immediately makes this matter known to Esther. She, in turn, alerts the king to this sinister plot; he narrowly averts his assassination. Esther credits Mordecai as the source of this information. However, the king fails to honor or even acknowledge Mordecai's act of courage.

Mordecai is overlooked. Perhaps you can relate! Mom, I'm taking a break from this story to affirm and encourage you. You, dear momma, are doing a great job! Although what you do seems to be largely unappreciated and much of it goes unnoticed, I take this opportunity to thank you for the countless ways you serve the Lord by serving your family. I hasten to remind you that while your family may not take note of all you do, your Heavenly Father is keeping accurate records of your good works. Hebrews 6:10 says, *For God is not unjust so as to forget your work and the love which you have shown toward His name, in having ministered and in still ministering to the saints.* Only in eternity will you reap your rewards for all the sacrifices of service you graciously bestowed on your little flock. In that day the Father will bless you and reward you. Trust me; it will be worth it all! We long to hear Jesus say, *"Well done, good and faithful slave. You were faithful with a few things, I will put you in charge of many things, enter into the joy of your master"* (Matt. 25:21). That will be the day!

God is keeping the books. If you faithfully commit to become the woman that God would have you to be, you will be blessed in this life and rewarded in the next.

**1. Look up Matthew 10:42. What great nugget of truth and encouragement can we receive from this verse?

_____

Mothering is a holy occupation. God faithfully records every act of kindness that is extended to a child. Isn't that great news?

The life of a godly woman will be punctuated by acts of benevolence. Our lives are to be a series of *"good works, as befits women making a claim to godliness"* (1 Tim. 2:10). Good works are the hallmark of every child of God. They cannot get you into heaven, but I urge you to leave a trail of them as you make your way there.

**2. Read 1 Timothy 5:9-10. Here Paul addresses the qualifications of a godly older woman. Make a list of the Christlike qualities for which we are to strive in our Christian lives.

_____

_____

A trail of good works is to be a natural outworking of a life under the control and influence of the Holy Spirit. I have developed a philosophy of life based on the Word of God. I treat my own family like very precious and important guests in my home. Guests in my home are treated like family. I want my family members to know they are very special and deserve my best. When I have guests, I want them to feel relaxed and at home. This outlook has worked well in our family!

Good works represent nothing more than faith in action. Doctrinally correct belief will manifest itself in godly behavior. John writes, *"The one who does not love his brother whom he has seen, cannot love God whom he has not seen"* (1 John 4:20). Love one another. Serve one another with gladness!

3. Read Paul's instructions to Timothy in 1 Timothy 6:18-19. According to this passage what is the essence of a life lived to the glory of God?

_____

Dear mom, you may be thinking that no one really cares or appreciates all the diligent work you invest in your children or in keeping your home nice. While in this life you may never get the affirmation you deserve, in eternity God will reward you. As you train up your children and meet the needs of your husband, do it as a love gift to your Heavenly Father. Not only will He be pleased, but you will be blessed. Your attitude toward the monotonous chores of daily life will be radically changed as you view your family as your personal mission field. Learn to see your role as a divine assignment from God the Father.

A queen does not require affirmation to do the right thing. She is ruled internally by the Holy Spirit. She is guided externally by the Word of God. She lives to please her King and not for the approval of her subjects.

Mordecai saves the king's life. That certainly is an admirable act of courage that should have been recognized and rewarded. When Mordecai does not get what he deserves, he does not become angry or bitter. He merely continues to entrust himself to the One *who judges righteously* (1 Pet. 2:23). Mordecai's selfless act that appears to go unnoticed is about to be rewarded.

A Nocturnal Nuisance

Read Esther 6:1-14

Insomnia is a bothersome ailment. In the Book of Esther this nocturnal nuisance is used to promote God's purpose and plan. The king cannot sleep. Like most who occasionally suffer from this malady, he decides to do some reading to relax and drift off to sleep. Little does King Ahasuerus know God is silently selecting his reading material and that the course of history will be altered this very night!

**1. Read Esther 6:1-3. When the king cannot sleep, he requests the book of records. That should put anyone to sleep. What does his reading material reveal?

_____

King Ahasuerus could not imagine how such an act of bravery could be overlooked. The king wants to discuss this glaring oversight with someone in his cabinet. He needs to discuss the best way to honor such a courageous act. He asks his staff to locate a member of the court. Haman, by God's design, is in the outer court. He is on a mission to speak to the king about hanging the very man the king intends to honor! Don't you just love how God works? The eye of faith if necessary to see God's hand in the outline of our lives, but if you look long enough, you will see Him. What a comforting thought!

In the midst of your grief or crisis you may feel as though God has abandoned you, but the Word of God assures you of His continual presence. We are His priceless treasures; He has promised to never fail us. Hebrews 13:5 says, _He Himself has said, "I will never desert you, nor will I ever forsake you."_ In Matthew 10:29 Jesus asks, _"Are not two sparrows sold for a cent? And yet not one of them will fall to the ground apart from your Father."_ God loves the sparrows and watches over them. How much more valuable are you to Him?

I am an amateur photographer. I love to contemplate my world through the viewfinder of my camera. After developing my pictures, I scrapbook my memories. The volume of patterned scrap paper generated by this hobby led me to a secondary hobby. I use the scraps to make my own stationery. My daughter-in-law, Patti, asked if she could use some of my leftover paper to make cards. I assured her she was welcome to use anything in my paper stash. She tentatively made a few selections but seemed hesitant to take much. I urged her to help herself. "I don't feel right helping myself to your supplies," she replied. "Patti," I reasoned, "You can have all you want. I have given you my son. Do you think I am going to draw the line at paper?"

God would say the same to us. "I have given you My Son. What good thing would I withhold from you?" Paul writes, *He who did not spare His own Son, but delivered Him over for us all, how will He not also with Him freely give us all things?* (Rom. 8:32). We are foolish when we doubt His presence just because we cannot see His face or trace His hand in our circumstances.

**2. God's Word assures us of God's continual care. Read Matthew 6:25-34. What insight can you gain from this passage?

_____

What is God's cure for anxious thoughts?

_____

How can you teach your children this important truth?

_____

In the midst of dire straits Mordecai continues to walk by faith. He spends time praying and fasting for the deliverance of his people. Little does he know that God is about to dramatically display His power on behalf of His people.

**3. Read Esther 6:6-9. When the king questions Haman about the best way to honor a hero, proud Haman assumes he is the object of the king's affection. What is Haman's response to the king?

_____

_____

_____

Proverbs 16:7 says, *When a man's ways are pleasing to the Lord, He makes even his enemies to be at peace with him.* Do not fear nor be dismayed. God will prevail.

The plot thickens. The noose tightens. Stay tuned for the exciting conclusion!

Weekly Summary

Please record insights gleaned from this week's study.

A Humble Hero

Read Esther 6:1-14

Proverbs 27:1 says, *"Do not boast about tomorrow, for you do not know what a day may bring forth."* If only Haman understood this radical truth!

At daybreak Haman rushes into the palace. He intends to have an early audience with the king to rid himself of his enemy, Mordecai. Suddenly he discovers the king is calling for him. Imagine Haman's burgeoning pride as he hastens towards the king. "This is the day about which I have been dreaming. I shall finally get what I deserve," Haman thinks as his steps quicken and his heart races with eager anticipation.

So Haman came in and the king said to him, "What is to be done for the man whom the king desire to honor?" And Haman said to himself, "Whom would the king desire to honor more than me?" (Esth. 6:6) Haman assumes the king is talking about honoring him. Who else deserves such respect and reverence? Whom else will the king want to honor but Haman? The thought the king might possibly be referring to another individual does not cross Haman's mind. His noxious pride has inflated his opinion of himself until it eclipses all others. Haman quickly recites a well-rehearsed list of tributes worthy of a man of his sterling character. Of course Haman thinks he is writing his own ticket to fame and fortune! *Then the king said to Haman, "Take quickly the robes and the horse as you have said, and do so for Mordecai the Jew, who is sitting at the king's gate; do not fall short in anything of all that you have said"* (Esth. 6:10). At the king's words, the air is sucked from Haman's lung; he struggles to breathe. "Mordecai," Haman stutters. "Did you say Mordecai? King Ahasuerus, did I hear you correctly? You want to honor Mordecai the Jew?"

Use your sanctified imagination for a moment and conjure up this scene in your mind. Picture this. The blood drains from Haman's face at the proclamation of the king. His jaw muscles clench reflexively. His pupils dilate in disgust; his eyes narrow into slits as he stares in disbelief at the king. His left eye twitches. He bites the inside of his jaw to prevent a vile profusion of words from exploding from his throat. The blood vessels in his neck bulge and pulsate with displaced anger. His breath emerges in short spurts as his blood pressure escalates rapidly. He is developing a dull headache in the base of his neck. The fingers of pain are beginning to travel around his head until they meet and join into an explosion of pain in his temples and spread across his forehead. His stomach cramps as it produces a spasm of acid which splashes up into his throat until he can literally taste his own hatred toward that miserable Jew named Mordecai. His knees buckle and nearly fail him as the weight of the king's words bear down on him. His head swims as the name of his archenemy sears into his brain and pierces his consciousness. He sways as if to faint and steadies himself by placing a trembling hand on the king's ornate desk. This scene is so rich with divine irony that it is absolutely delicious!

Haman has no choice but to obey the king. Haman remembers Queen Vashti's fate. People seem to disappear or die for acts of subversion or insubordination. Haman only has one option. His ego deflates like a leaking helium balloon. A humiliated Haman leaves the king's presence in search of Mordecai.

Haman finds Mordecai. He chokes on his word as he relays the king's intentions. *So Haman took the robe and the horse, and arrayed Mordecai, and led him on horseback through the city square, and proclaimed before him, "Thus it shall be done to the man whom the king desires to honor"* (Esth. 6:11). A pale and drawn Haman leads the mighty royal steed on which Mordecai rides. With tight-lipped disdain Haman hoarsely proclaims the king's message.

**1. Reread Esther 6:12. What does Mordecai do after the king lavishes praise and honor on him?

The true measure of a man is how he deals with promotion and praise. Mordecai reveals his genuine humility by returning to his normal routine. Neither fame, nor fortune, nor sudden celebrity will alter Mordecai's calling. He continues to serve in his former capacity with a gentle and contrite spirit. Mordecai returns to the king's gate. He returns to life as usual.

Before we leave this episode, let me point out several things. Mordecai is honored for doing the right thing. When he discovers a plot to assassinate the king, he makes the plan known to Esther. The villains are arrested and executed. Mordecai saves the king's life, but his act of bravery is somehow overlooked. Notice he does not seek commendation. He continues living his life and walking in truth and righteousness. His act of bravery is not motivated by reward or recognition. Doing right has its own reward.

Pursing a life that is well-pleasing to the Lord will result in soul satisfaction. In Psalm 16: 11 David writes, *You will make known to me the path of life; in Your presence is fullness of joy; in Your right hand there are pleasures forever.* As members of the royal family we seek the affirmation of the King of Glory.

Mom, teach your children to do the right thing even when no one is looking. Teach them to walk in integrity and truth. Proverbs 4:20-23 says, *My son, give attention to my words; incline your ear to my sayings. Do not let them depart from your sight; keep them in the midst of your heart. For they are life to those who find them, and health to all their whole body.* Watch over your heart with all diligence, for from it flow the springs of life. Be diligent to train up your children in the way they should go. Teach them God's Word; demonstrate a godly lifestyle. Your actions actually will speak louder than your words.

2. Look up Matthew 7:13-14. Note the contrast between the path of righteousness and the way to destruction. Write down your insight.

_____

The path of righteousness is a narrow pathway that runs contrary to the ways of the world. In a world gone mad, training your children according to God's Holy Word is imperative. Rear them according to scriptural principles. Teach the intrinsic value of integrity.

Mordecai does the right thing without expectations of reward. In time he is honored for his act of bravery and courage.

**3. In fact, this type of self-promotion is condemned in the Bible. Read Matthew 6:1-6. How does Jesus instruct his disciples in regard to righteous living?

_____

What can we learn from this passage?

_____

A surrendered heart motivates personal holiness. God will bless you for living a life of personal holiness and practical righteousness. He may even choose to exalt you in this lifetime for your good works. However, rest assured that God is keeping account of every good deed and that they will not go unnoticed. Either in this life or in the next, reward will follow righteousness.

**4. Look up Hebrews 6:10. What a powerful promise! What does this verse tell us about our Righteous Judge?

_____

Be encouraged, sweet mom. Every act of kindness done in the name of Jesus will be rewarded either on earth or in heaven. Keep pressing on! Matthew 6:20 says, *But lay up for yourselves treasures in heaven, where neither moth nor rust doth corrupt, and where thieves do not break through or steal* (KJV). May your goal be to please the Lord.

After leading Mordecai around the city square, Haman slithers home as he snivels and whines to his bewildered wife about his situation. Before he can collect his thoughts, he hears a knock at the door. Haman is swept out of the house and escorted to Esther's banquet. Little does he know his terrible, awful, no-good, very bad day is about to go from bad to worse!

An Enemy Exposed

Read Esther 7:1-10

Esther is the epitome of grace under pressure. Her thoughts are consumed with the impending annihilation of herself, her beloved cousin, and her Jewish brethren. In the midst of her conflicted emotions she exhibits the grace and courage of a seasoned child of God. She reminds me of the virtuous woman to whom Proverbs 31:25 refers when it says, *Strength and dignity are her clothing, and she smiles at the future.* Even though the current circumstances are daunting, Esther's trust is firmly rooted in God. She is not afraid of what the future holds.

Knowledge of the sentence of death on every Jew does not force Esther to act inappropriately. She is committed to waiting patiently on God's timing to make her request known to the king. We wrestle with the concept of waiting. We are locked into a world that whirls about at a maddening pace. We live a life that is marked by minutes, hours, days, weeks, and months. Most of us operate from day-planners that dictate our demanding routine. Appointments, activities, engagements, and commitments dominate our time. We wonder how we will ever get it all done! We race from one activity to another. We eat fast food in route and change clothes in the car. A leisurely home-cooked meal has become a rarity in the American culture. Even we as Christians have fallen prey to the hustle and bustle of our hurried society.

Time moves fast. God, however, is not constrained by time. God has no night. God has no day. He probably does not wear a watch; I don't think He owns a calendar. As the great I Am He has no past, present, or future. He operates in a dimension that transcends time as we know it. While we view life as a series of still shots linked together by the continuum of time, He sees all of our lives all at once. A fascinating verse in Ecclesiastes 3:15 states, *That which is has been already and that which will be has already been, for God seeks what has passed by.* The past, the present, and the future are alike to God. Consequently, time is of no importance to God. Timing, however, is everything to the Lord. Esther knows this truth. She is not rushing ahead of God, nor is she panicked by her dire straits. Nor is she lagging behind. She does not hamper the Lord's work with a cynical attitude of despair and defeat.

When God does not seem to be working fast enough to suit our predetermined schedule, we often are tempted to bypass His providence and initiate our own plan. This is a waste of valuable emotional energy and can be spiritually dangerous.

**1. Look up Isaiah 50:11. Here the Bible warns us about attempting to build our own fire. What are the results of self-effort?

_____

Learning to wait on the Lord is perhaps one of the most difficult lessons of the Christian life. The tendency is to create a plan of our own. The flurry of the activity alone makes us feel better, but the end result will be disastrous.

2. The key to successfully waiting on the Lord is to stay quietly in His presence until we get clear directions from Him. Look up Isaiah 26:3-4. What does this verse say?

_____

The more we stay focused on the Lord Jesus, the more we are able to discern His subtle movements in our lives. A sensitive heart is required to detect these changes. In the mystery of God's timing, in His subtle movements, in the quiet, still, small voice of His Spirit, we sense His presence. This is the role wisdom, based on the Word of God, plays in life. The subdued heart and the surrendered spirit respond to the slightest touch of the Father. Esther exemplifies this reality as she waits on the Lord for His direction.

The king once again questions Esther about her matter of concern. He offers her up to half of the kingdom to satisfy her need. This was a common gesture to denote generosity and not an actual measure. At any rate, Esther feels the gentle prompting of the Spirit of God. The time to speak has arrived. Ecclesiastes 3:1,7a says, _There is a time for every event under heaven . . . a time to be silent, and a time to speak._

Learning the restraint of the Spirit is every bit as important as is learning the release of the Spirit. That is, silence is a virtue. Sadly, most of us run our mouths without engaging our brains!

**3. Look up Proverbs 10:19. What does this verse teach?

_____

What a timely verse for us to memorize and practice! Most of us talk too much!

**4. In James 1:19 what does James advise?

_____

We would all do well to follow this admonition from the Word of God. Be quick to hear the Spirit of God. Be slow to speak. In the midst of our prattle, transgression is nearly impossible to avoid. Be slow to anger. Don't jump to conclusions. Listen to the Spirit of God and ponder how to respond. Learn to speak words of grace seasoned with salt. Ephesians 4:29 says, _Let no unwholesome word proceed from your mouth, but only such a word as is good for edifi-_

cation according to the need of the moment, so that it will give grace to those who hear. A queen knows how to speak properly and develops the fine art of listening. She speaks for the monarchy, so she carefully chooses her words. She guards her tone of voice. She is cautious with her body language. She considers herself an ambassador for the royal family; she conducts herself accordingly.

With diplomacy and sensitivity Esther reveals her heart to her husband. Esther says, "*A foe and an enemy is this wicked Haman!*" *Then Haman became terrified before the king and queen* (Esth. 7:6). God lives in a spiritual realm that transcends our temporal world. He is invincible. When He moves, He is awesome in power and splendid in might.

A False Friend

Read Esther 7:1-10

Esther's revelation of Haman's betrayal stuns King Ahasuerus. Haman is the king's trusted advisor and confidant. The king promotes him to prime minister and gives him the signet ring. How can such a loyal friend betray the bonds of trust? The king is victim of friendly fire.

The king reacts angrily at Esther's implication of Haman. *And the king arose in his anger from drinking wine and went into the palace garden* (Esth. 7:7a). The king is so startled by the sudden turn of events that he storms out of the banqueting hall. He walks briskly toward the royal gardens to clear his bewildered head and to gain control over his swirling thoughts.

King Ahasuerus begins to sort through the jumbled facts and processes recent events. How can this happen? How can his queen and her people be under the sentence of death without his knowledge of the matter? How has he misjudged Haman's character? How has the edict to annihilate the Jewish people passed through his hands without making any impact on him? How has he signed off on such an evil deed without questioning Haman's judgment? The king knows to a certain extent that he is implicated, but how does this happen?

The king may not be able to recall the exact circumstances that lead up to the edict. Who knows how many official papers Ahasuerus signed that day? Haman may have even buried his edict amidst stacks of other papers awaiting the king's signature. The king may have signed it without giving it a great deal of attention. The king has countless decisions to make and a myriad of pressing legislative needs to address.

King Ahasuerus has trusted Haman implicitly. Haman has betrayed the king's trust to promote his own agenda. Perhaps no hurt runs as deep as the betrayal of a friend.

**1. David certainly understands this kind of betrayal. Read Psalm 35:11-16. Although he treats these people as if they are family, how do they repay his kindness?

As Christians, we are not surprised when one outside the faith proves to be untrustworthy. When the wounds originate from within the family of God by a trusted friend and confidante, the pain of friendly fire is nearly unbearable. In Psalm 41:9 David writes, *Even my close friend in whom I trusted, who ate my bread, has lifted up his heel against me.* Betrayal at the hands of an enemy is painful; betrayal at the hands of a friend is unthinkable.

2. In Psalm 55:12-14 David again addresses this situation. Describe the relationship David has with the one who betrays him.

You can feel David's agony as he pens these words of disappointment. David knows the excruciating pain of friendly fire. No one has ever known the depth of this kind of betrayal like our Lord Jesus does. Betrayal of the most heinous kind emanates from one of the Twelve.

**3. Read John 6:70-71. What does Jesus say about Judas?

From the beginning Jesus knows the identity of the one amongst His disciples who will betray Him. At the Last Passover Jesus says, *"Truly I say to you that one of you will betray Me"* (Matt. 26:21). The disciples are stunned and say, "Surely not I, Lord?" *And He answered, "He who dipped his hand with Me in the bowl is the one who will betray Me. The Son of Man is to go, just as it is written of Him; but woe to that man by whom the Son of Man is betrayed! It would have been good for that man if he had not been born"* (Matt. 26:24). In His Incarnation the Lord experiences the betrayal of a friend.

4. The sheer fact of Judas's betrayal is painful, but his method of identifying the Lord Jesus is doubly painful. Read Matthew 26:47-49. How does Judas confirm to His captors the identity of Jesus Christ?

Judas betrays the Lord with a kiss. How cruel! Although Jesus knows that the devil has *already put into the heart of Judas Iscariot, the son of Simon, to betray Him* (John 113:2b) the searing pain of Judas' infidelity surely adds to the unspeakable pain of the cross. We can be confident the Lord Jesus understands our pain when we experience friendly fire.

King Ahasuerus has been betrayed by Haman, his closest advisor. As the king paces among the manicured beds in the royal gardens, he is scarcely aware of the rich fragrance emitted by the rare and costly plantings. He does not notice the sculpted shrubbery. The treachery of a friend and the ramifications of the deadly edict occupy his mind.

One last thought to ponder. When heartache invades our lives, we often jump to the conclusion God has somehow abandoned us. Learn this. God may be silent, but He is not absent. He is constantly at work. When you cannot trace His hand, trust His heart! He stands in the wings, silently monitoring the situation and orchestrating the circumstances. Romans 8:28 reminds us, *And we know that God causes all things to work together for good to those who love God, to those who are called according to His purpose.* Beloved, rest in God's sovereign purpose and plan for your life. Trust in Him alone.

A Just Judgment

Read Esther 7:1-10

Craig and I live in a rural area outside Memphis. Recently I was driving on our country roads and happened on a loathsome gathering of buzzards. About 10 of the large creatures stood in a circle and dined on the remains of an animal that had met an unfortunate end. Their heads were bent low; their wings were tightly folded at their sides. Their beady eyes and hooked beaks combined to create a sinister appearance. As I watched the disgusting sight, I could not help but think of Satan and his minions. Satan has a highly organized army of demons he can dispatch at any moment. Unleashed on an unsuspecting person, they are able to wreak havoc and then fiendishly feast on the resulting destruction. Satan is using Haman to institute his plan for the destruction of God's chosen people. On the surface, evil appears to be able to overcome good.

While the name of God never is mentioned in the Book of Esther, His presence certainly is evident. Close inspection of the story of Esther reveals His fingerprints. Many of God's displays of power in the Old Testament are awesome in scope. Fire, thunder, lightning, and earthquakes accompany His presence. In the Book of Esther, God's movement is veiled; His nuances are subtle.

Just as in Esther's day God still reigns. He is accomplishing His divine purpose and plan. Even when we cannot understand Him, even when He seems to defy logical explanation, even when His ways are contrary to our finely laid plans, God is faithful. We can trust Him to work all things together for our good and His glory. What a glorious truth we can learn from the little Book of Esther!

Haman never knows what hits him. A short time before he is bragging and boasting to his wife and friends about his power and prestige. Soon after his recital of his personal accomplishments, he is called into a private audience with the king. The king wants some advice on how to honor someone. Haman immediately assumes the king is about to publicly exalt him. Haman has a list of trinkets he would like. He soon discovers the king is talking about honoring Mordecai, not Haman! Talk about your reversal of fortune! Suddenly Haman finds himself trumpeting the praises of Mordecai throughout the city of Susa. How does this happen?

After that humiliating event Haman goes home to lick his wounds. No sooner has he arrived home than the king's guards appear to personally usher him to a private banquet with the king and queen. Haman's head is swimming. His mind is racing. If Haman thinks his day could not possibly get any worse, he is sadly mistaken! Queen Esther identifies Haman as the culprit behind the impending annihilation of her people.

Exit the king stage left. The king is so furious, he has to leave the room lest his explosive anger cause him to fall on Haman and tear him limb from limb. Haman is terrified and *stayed to beg for his life from Queen Esther, for he saw that harm had been determined against him by the king* (Esth. 7:7). The noose tightens.

Haman begs for mercy. He falls on Queen Esther's couch and claws at her royal robes in a desperate effort to sway her to speak to the king on his behalf and spare his life. The king appears in the doorway. *"Will you assault the queen with me in the house?"* (Esth. 7:8), spat the king, whose anger toward Haman knows no bounds.

**1.The king's servant steps forward and suggests a just judgment for Haman. Reread Esther 7:9-10. What is his suggestion?

_____

If Satan has ever attempted to cause you to doubt God's sovereign control over His creation, surely this episode in Esther gives you the basis to reconsider the claims of Christ. Of Christ, in Ephesians 1:20-23 Paul writes that God *raised Him from the dead, and seated Him at His right hand in the heavenly places, far above all rule and authority and power and dominion, and every name that is named, not only in this age, but also in the one to come. And He put all things in subjection under His feet, and gave Him as head over all things to the church, which is His body, the fullness of Him who fills all in all.* Christ is the ruler of all. All things are subject to His power and His authority. As we learn to rest in that truth, we begin to live like queens!

In Christ, God has given us *kingdom authority*. This is not religious rhetoric; kingdom authority is available to every child of God. Kingdom authority is available, but it is not automatic. God's power is appropriated by obedience to the Word of God, dependence on the Spirit of God, and confidence in the Son of God. God will not empower a disobedient child any more than you would reward rebellion in your child. He is looking for a heart that is wholly His to endow with resurrection power.

2. Read Ephesians 1:17-19. Paul records his prayer for us. What does Paul pray for all of us?

_____

_____

_____

Paul wants us to understand the power that has been granted to us as children of God. We are a part of the heavenly monarchy. We have been given *the surpassing greatness of His power as our inheritance in Him* (see Eph. 1:18-19). He has qualified us to be joint heirs with

Jesus (Rom. 8:17) and empowered us to live above the downward pull of the flesh. No longer are we helpless captives of sin, self, and Satan (Rom. 6:11-14). We can crucify (Gal. 2:20) the contrary thoughts of the world, the flesh, and the devil. We can take every thought captive to the obedience of Christ (2 Cor. 10:3-5). By faith we can yield ourselves to the Holy Spirit and allow Him to produce the sweet fragrant aroma of Christ in us (2 Cor. 2:15).

**3. One blessing of the Christian life is found in Galatians 5:16-24. We no longer carry out the desire of the flesh. What are the deeds of the flesh?

_____

_____

_____

In Christ we are dead to sin and alive to Him. When we walk in obedience to Christ, He produces His fruit in our lives. List the fruit of the Spirit. Ask God to create in you these lovely characteristics of Christ.

_____

_____

_____

We have been placed as royal members of the kingdom of God. As such, we are to learn to live like queens.

In a sweeping move of providence, God ordains the circumstances of Esther's life. *For such a time as this* she was promoted to the palace to intercede on behalf of her people. For a period of time evil appears as though it will prevail, but not so.

One of the king's eunuchs said, *"Behold indeed, the gallows standing at Haman's house fifty cubits high, which Haman made for Mordecai who spoke good on behalf of the king!" And the king said, "Hang him on it." So they hanged Haman on the gallows which he had prepared for Mordecai, and the king's anger subsided* (Esth. 7:9-10). Haman is hanged on the very gallows that he has prepared for Mordecai. What divine irony! The psalmist writes, *For without cause they hid their net for me; without cause they dug a pit for my soul. Let destruction come upon him unawares; and let the net which he hid catch himself; into that very destruction let him fall* (Ps. 35:7-8). Haman is caught in his own net.

The Potter's Piece

Read Esther 8:1-17

None of us knows what the future holds for our families. Wisdom dictates that we make plans, but learn this about the Lord: At any time God may chose to override our carefully laid plans and interrupt our lives. He certainly has that right; He often uses His prerogative to disrupt our well-orchestrated lives and to stir our nest.

1. Read James 4:13-15. James describes how to live. In this passage what does he tell us about the brevity of life?

_____

Taking care of your physical body as if you are going to live forever is wise. Take care of your spiritual being as if you are going to die tomorrow and give an account of your earthly deeds. Plan for the future, but at any moment be ready to meet Jesus without regrets.

If you knew that tomorrow would be your last day, would you change anything about the way you are living? If so, do some spiritual inventory. In 2 Corinthians 5:9 Paul says, *Therefore we also have as our ambition, whether at home or absent, to be pleasing to Him.* That sums up the essence of the Christian life. In Philippians 1:21-24 Paul says, *For to me, to live is Christ, and to die is gain. But I am hard-pressed from both directions, having the desire to depart, and be with Christ, for that is very much better, yet to remain on in the flesh is more necessary for your sake.* Whether we are here on earth or in glory, our goal is to be well pleasing to the Lord Jesus Christ.

As Christians we belong to the Lord. First Corinthians 3:16 says, *Do you not know that you are a temple of God, and that the Spirit of God dwells in you?* We have been bought with a terrible price; we belong to the Lord. He has every right to direct our lives as He sees fit.

**2. Read Romans 9:20-21. Describe Paul's analogy and the meaning behind it.

_____

From this brief passage what can you learn about God's plan for our lives?

_____

Why do we so often resist the gentle touch of the Potter when He attempts to mold and make us into His image?

Several years ago I attended a women's conference in Georgia. A Christian potter did several vignettes to illustrate the spiritual truth of the potter and the clay. In one demonstration the potter sat at his wheel patiently working a lump of clay. With each rotation of the wheel we marveled at the transformation of the clay. Using water to keep the clay pliable, the potter applied equal amounts of pressure to the outside and the inside of the vessel. As he envisioned the finished product, he patiently worked the clay into the desired shape. As he worked, he told how his continual touch on the clay allowed him to detect the slightest imperfection in the clay. If undetected even one granule of sand could weaken the finished product. It would spoil the esthetics of the piece as well as cheapen its value. I noticed that his back was bent over the wheel and his face was very close to the clay as he worked to create a piece that was both lovely to look at and practical for use. His diligence with the clay and his masterful creativity soon produced a wonderful pitcher from what had been a formless lump of clay. Lifting his hands from the finished piece, he noted the amount of clay that was smeared on his hands from working the piece into completion. As he showed the audience his palms, he said, "When the potter is in the process of molding the piece, he is intimately acquainted with the clay." I will never forget the mental imagery those words evoked in my spirit. As God sits at His potter's wheel, He is leaning over me with His face close to His masterpiece. He is intimately acquainted with every detail of my life!

As a lump of clay in the nail-scarred hands of the Master Potter, my only wise option is to surrender to His gentle touch and become conformed to the image of Christ. Isaiah 64:8 says, *But now, O Lord, You are our Father, we are the clay, and You our potter, and all of us are the work of Your hand.* When God is left undisturbed to work at His potter's wheel, a vessel fit for the King is created out of a lump of useless clay.

Esther is a lovely example of this marvelous truth. The sovereignty of God moved her from poverty to the palace, from rags to riches, from brokenness to blessedness. God places her in a place of influence and authority. Had you stopped reading Esther midway, you might have been convinced evil triumphs over good. Wicked Haman has been promoted to the position of prime minister. King Ahasuerus has unwisely given Haman his signet ring. Haman is using his unlimited power to exterminate the Jewish race corporately and Mordecai individually. Now, for the rest of the story!

After Esther risks her own life by speaking to the king without an invitation, she reveals Haman's cruel plot to the king. The king immediately has Haman executed on the very gallows Haman has constructed for Mordecai. The king gives Haman's estate to Esther. She, in turn, gives it to Mordecai. Good triumphs over evil.

God has written into His creation a divine principle that we refer to as *the law of the harvest.*

**3. Read Galatians 6:7-8. According to this passage, what is *the law of the harvest*?

_____

How does the Book of Esther demonstrate this?

_____

God is keeping meticulous records. From our limited perspective, evil may appear to be winning. Rest assured God will even the score. God will not allow evil to go unpunished. Ultimately, God's divine purposes will be accomplished. Fix your eyes on Jesus; keep living like a queen!

Weekly Summary

Please record insights gleaned from this week's study.

A Sudden Situation

Read Esther 8:1-17

For nearly 30 years I have walked with God. I gladly attest to the fact that He is faithful. In 2 Timothy 2:11-13 Paul says, *It is a trustworthy statement: for if we died with Him, we shall also live with Him; if we endure, we will also reign with Him; if we deny Him, He also will deny us; if we are faithless, He remains faithful; for He cannot deny Himself.* God is faithful. In the dark night season of the soul, we are tempted to feel abandoned and alone. Wait for the Lord. Trust in the sovereign work of God. He will manifest His presence. In His timing, God's glory will descend and eclipse our troubled souls.

Throughout nearly 34 years of marriage, Craig and I have faced many black nights of despair and sorrow. Grief, heartache, and pain are the traveling companions of every child of God. In this fallen world, the universal result is sin, suffering, and sorrow. We will not escape pain in this sin-sick planet. In dark moments, God faithfully makes His presence known. We experience Him gently speaking a word of peace to our troubled souls. Isaiah 40:11 says, *Like a shepherd He will tend His flock, in His arm He will gather the lambs, and carry them in His bosom; He will gently lead the nursing ewes.* God tenderly looks to the needs of His people.

As Craig and I have faced down some dark days of suffering and grief in our lives, we have learned to trust the Lord. In some situations He has calmed the storm around us. In others He has not removed the difficulty, but He has tenderly comforted us in the midst of the storm. Grace gives us the spiritual fortitude to face any battle and emerge victorious. We may be tattered and scarred, but we will win the victory because of Calvary!

God stands strong on Esther's behalf. *On that day King Ahasuerus gave the house of Haman the enemy of the Jews, to Queen Esther; and Mordecai came before the king, for Esther had disclosed what he was to her* (Esth. 8:1). The laws of the Medes and the Persians say that a condemned criminal's property reverts to the crown. The king gives Esther Haman's estate. *Esther revealed her relationship to Mordecai, who stood before the king. The king took off his signet ring which he had taken away from Haman, and gave it to Mordecai. And Esther set Mordecai over the house of Haman.* In a dramatic reversal, Mordecai is vested with the authority previously belonging to Haman. He is given Haman's possessions. Ironically, Mordecai is granted all the power and property Haman previously holds.

Esther faces an impossible situation. All hope is gone until suddenly God moves. On the surface God appears to be uninvolved. On the surface evil appears to be about to overcome righteousness. Suddenly God moves. While God is always engaged behind the scenes, He often suddenly breaks into our reality with the power of His presence. Living in the reality of God's sovereignty requires faith. It affords us the luxury of resting in God's providence and waiting on His "suddenly" moment.

**1. Read Luke 2:8-14. Suddenly eternity intrudes on history. What happens suddenly?

_____

The birth of Jesus is heralded by the sudden appearance of an angel of the Lord. Suddenly everything changes.

**2. Look at Luke 24:1-5. What event suddenly transpires at the empty tomb?

_____

Two heavenly heralds suddenly accompany the resurrection of Jesus.

**3. Read Acts 2:1-2. The disciples await Pentecost when the Holy Spirit would descend and indwell believers. What event suddenly happens?

_____

The arrival of the blessed Holy Spirit suddenly is ushered in with the sound of a rushing wind.

God moves suddenly on our behalf. He is always engaged, but often He suddenly moves in great power. His undeniable presence intrudes on our reality. Suddenly God appears. As a member of His royal family, be prepared for His sudden interruptions into your life.

4. Read Matthew 25:1-13. The parable of the 10 virgins illustrates this point. How does the Lord characterize the 10 women?

_____

The bridegroom suddenly appears. What happens next?

_____

How can we live in a state of preparedness for the Lord's return?

_____

We are expected to live in a state of readiness. The Lord will return. We want to be found faithfully working for the cause of Christ when He suddenly appears. _For the Lord Himself will descend from heaven with a shout, with the voice of the archangel and with the trumpet of God, and the dead in Christ will rise first. Then we who are alive and remain will be caught up together with them in the clouds to meet the Lord in the air, and so we shall always be with the Lord_ (1 Thess. 4:16-17).When He appears, we do not want to shrink back in shame. We want to hear Jesus say, "Well done."

A Joyous Jubilation

Read Esther 8:1-17

Esther faces an enemy that seems impossible to defeat until God steps in and changes the outcome. The results are amazing. God changes the king's heart. King Ahasuerus is one of the most powerful men of his time. People live or die by the wave of his hand. Judgments are rendered by a nod of his head. Destinies are determined by his pen stroke. Yet God turns the heart of a Gentile king. *She obtained favor in his sight* (Esth. 5:2).

**1. Read Proverbs 21:1. Concerning the king's heart, what does this verse teach us?

_____

Is this verse conditional on the spiritual nature of the king or person in authority?

_____

By faith, Esther believes King Ahasuerus' heart is in God's hand. She trusts God to work in a pagan palace. She believes He can use even lost people and the evil intentions of a man like Haman to serve His purposes. Beloved, this is a powerful truth for those of us committed to living in God's sovereignty. We can trust God to move in the shadows of our circumstances. He is capable of turning hearts and overriding impossible situations to orchestrate His perfect plan.

With Haman executed and Mordecai wearing the king's signet ring, at least part of the wrong has been made right. However, the edict that will annihilate the Jews still is in effect. The Law of the Medes and Persians cannot be changed.

Then Esther spoke again to the king, fell at his feet, wept, and implored him to avert the evil scheme of Haman the Agagite and his plan which he had devised against the Jews (Esth. 8:3). Esther is grateful that she and Mordecai are spared. However, her people remain under the sentence of death. Esther cries out, *"How can I endure to see the calamity which will befall my people, and how can I endure to see the destruction of my kindred?"* (Esth. 8:6).

The spiritual parallel demonstrated for us is one of intercessory prayer for those outside a personal relationship with Christ. Esther is not satisfied to live while her brethren are systematically executed. She longs for them to know the grace she has received. What a glorious picture of an intercessor! May her example challenge us to intercede with weeping, fasting, and prayer on behalf of those who do not know Christ.

Second Corinthians 5:18-19 says, *Now all these things are from God, who reconciled us to Himself through Christ, and gave us the ministry of reconciliation, namely, that God was in Christ reconciling the world to Himself, not counting their trespasses against them, and He committed to us the word of reconciliation.* God desires to use us as His partners in bringing others to Himself. Now that is a staggering thought!

All of us have family and friends who are outside Christ. How can we enjoy the bounty of blessings that accompany salvation without pleading on their behalf? Before the throne of grace call the names of those who are lost and dead in their transgressions and sin. Pray for these who seem unconcerned about the approaching Day of Judgment. We war against an enemy more wicked than Haman. Our enemy, the devil, prowls about like a roaring lion seeking whom he might devour. He has blinded the eyes of those who are without the Lord. Implore the Father to open their eyes of understanding and allow them to see the glorious salvation of our Lord!

Esther begs for the salvation of her kinsmen. King Ahasuerus' heart has softened toward Esther and the plight of the Jews, but he is powerless to reverse an edict written into the Law of the Medes and the Persians. The king cannot remove Haman's edict, but a law can be written that will neutralize his murderous intent. *The king said to Mordecai, "Now you write to the Jews as you see fit, in the king's name, and seal it with the king's signet ring; for a decree which is written in the name of the king and sealed with the king's signet ring may not be revoked"* (Esth. 8:8).

2. Read Esther 8:7-14. What does Mordecai's decree say?

_____

A copy of the edict to be issued as law in each and every province was published to all the peoples, so that the Jews would be ready for this day to avenge themselves on their enemies. The couriers, hastened and impelled by the king's command, went out, riding on the royal steeds; and the decree was given out at the citadel in Susa (Esth. 8:13-14).

The Jews are living under the sentence of death. Like a pall, dread hangs in the air. The rumble of approaching horses strikes fresh fear in their hearts. The last time they have heard the sound of thundering horse hooves, it has brought news of annihilation. Now what?

The Jewish people anxiously gather around the signpost to read the newly posted edict. The air, thick with clouds of dust kicked up by the king's couriers, catches in the throat of the Jews. They quickly scan the decree and mentally process the gist of the new law. Suddenly, cries of astonished relief split the heavy air as the Jews embrace loved ones. Tears of unbridled joy spill down their cheeks and make furrows in their dust-caked faces. God has made a way of escape. The Jews are given permission to defend themselves on the day of their destruction. Hope replaces horror. Pleasure replaces pain.

Again, a spiritual reality is glaringly obvious in this tiny Book of Esther. We also are born under a sentence of death. As sinners by birth, by choice, and by practice we are enemies of God the Father. Our sinful nature condemns us to death. We are hopeless and helpless. An immutable law of sin and death is instituted when Adam sins in the Garden of Eden. We are under a sentence of death being born in the likeness of Adam. The Law of the Medes and Persians cannot be revoked. However, God makes a way of escape through the cross and the shed blood of Jesus Christ. Romans 10:13 says, *Whoever will call on the name of the Lord will be saved.* Romans 8:2 says, *For the law of the Spirit of life in Christ Jesus has set you free from the law of sin and of death.* The law of grace supersedes the law of sin and death. Hallelujah! What a Savior!

As the copy of Esther's edict circulates, *the city of Susa shouted and rejoiced.* Esther 8:16-17 says, *For the Jews there was light and gladness and joy and honor. And in each and every province, and in each and every city, wherever the king's commandment and his decree arrived, there was gladness and joy for the Jews, a feast and a holiday. And many among the peoples of the land became Jews, for the dread of the Jews had fallen on them.* Psalm 30:5 says, *Weeping may last for the night, but a shout of joy comes in the morning.* How true that verse is to the Jews of Esther's day. God gives them *a garland instead of ashes, the oil of gladness instead of mourning, the mantle of praise instead of a spirit of fainting* (Isa. 61:3). The joy bells ring in Susa and in the surrounding provinces! What a day of rejoicing that must have been!

The unrestrained rejoicing and jubilation among the Jews attract others to the Lord. The spirit of joy in the life of a child of God is contagious. When others see the joy of the Lord that is our strength (Neh. 8:10), they become interested in what we have in Jesus Christ. Are the joy bells ringing in your heart? Does your life speak of the joy of the Lord that is our strength?

We are seated with Christ in heavenly places (Eph. 2:6). We are part of God's royal family. Our citizenship is in heaven. We reign in this life. As a member of the heavenly monarchy we demonstrate the joy of the Lord. We become winsome testimonies of the saving life of Christ. We are ready to make a defense to everyone who asks us *to give an account for the hope that is in us* (see 1 Pet. 3:15). We are reigning in real life!

A Formidable Foe

Read Esther 9:1-32

Anti-Semitic attitudes in the Persian Empire escalate to the boiling point as Haman's edict gives a voice to growing hatred for the Jews. God's sovereignty puts Esther in a place of authority *for such a time as this*. Her intercession prevents the senseless slaughter of thousands of Hebrews. King Ahasuerus does not have the power to reverse a decree once it is written into the law of the Medes and Persians. He does, however, have the authority to circumvent an edict by neutralizing it with a counter measure.

The king gives Mordecai the authority to write an edict to supersede the murderous intentions of Haman. Mordecai's decree allows the Jews to protect themselves against any who might attempt to do them harm.

The enemies of the Jews intend *to gain the mastery over them* on the day appointed by Haman's evil edict. Esther 9:1 says, *Now in the twelfth month (that is, the month Adar), on the thirteenth day when the king's command and edict were about to be executed, on the day when the enemies of the Jews hoped to gain the mastery over them, it was turned to the contrary so that the Jews themselves gained the mastery over those who hated them.* A door of deliverance swings open on the silent hinges of God's purpose and plan for the Jews!

**1. For a season evil appears to be winning, but ultimately righteousness will prevail. Read Psalm 37:7-15. According to this passage, what is the final outcome?

_____

In the meantime what are you and I to be doing?

_____

From these verses what can we learn?

_____

When the appointed day arrives, *the Jews assembled in their cites . . . and no one could stand before them, for the dread of them had fallen on all the peoples* (Esth. 9:2). The tables have turned. Under Haman's edict the Jews stand condemned. Now in light of Mordecai's decree the dread of the Jews has fallen on the people of Persia.

The Jews assemble to fight. Armed and standing shoulder-to-shoulder they vanquish their enemies. This imagery is not lost on us. In the Christian community we are called to be soldiers of the cross.

2. Read 2 Timothy 2:3-4. What example does Paul use to describe the Christian life?

_____

How does he describe the life of a soldier?

_____

As Christians we are called to *fight the good fight of faith* (1 Tim. 6:12). This conjures up the idea of a mighty army of warriors fighting for a common purpose.

**3. Read Ephesians 6:10-17. We are instructed to put on the whole armor of God. Why?

_____

If we were not in a battle, we would not need armor. We are called to be soldiers. Who is our enemy?

_____

List the pieces of armor and their purpose.

1.

2.

3.

4.

5.

6.

Salvation places us into the Lord's army. We are to join our brothers and sisters in the fray. Failure to do so leaves an unguarded position in the rank and gives the enemy access.

The Jews are assisted by the governmental officials. *Even all the princes of the provinces, the satraps, the governors and those who were doing the king's business assisted the Jews, because the dread of Mordecai had fallen on them. Indeed, Mordecai was great in the king's house, and his fame spread throughout all the provinces; for the man Mordecai became greater and greater* (Esth. 9:3-4). Before Esther's intercession with the king, the government likely would have aided in the annihilation of the Jews. Now with Haman executed and Mordecai exalted, the king's officials help the Jews battle their enemies.

The reputation of Mordecai spreads throughout the empire. He has been exalted to the very position Haman has occupied. The king has given Mordecai his signet ring, which is the symbol of his authority. Ownership of the ring indicates he is the most exalted of all the king's ministers. Mordecai's fame strikes fear in those who oppose the Jews and grants them victory over their enemies.

Haman is a formidable foe, but his evil intent can not overtake God's plan. We have a formidable foe. Satan, the prince of the power of the air, is set against the Lord and His church. He may appear to win some skirmishes, but he is the ruler of a doomed domain. Calvary seals his fate. Although Satan is a defeated foe, he remains very active. Using the subtleties of innuendoes and lies he continues to cast doubt on God and His Word. A believer without a renewed mind is his continual target. Only when we become proficient at rightly dividing the Word of God are we able to rout him. He goes about as a roaring lion looking for an unguarded believer to take captive with his lies. He is a conquered foe, but he remains quite formidable. At the end of the age he will be cast into the lake of fire.

Revelation 20:10 says, *And the devil who deceived them was thrown into the lake of fire and brimstone, where the beast and the false prophet are also; and they will be tormented day and night forever and ever.* Until that time, put on the whole armor of God and fight our aggressive enemy.

God's providence is the theme of the Book of Esther. God is at work behind the scenes. Although Haman and his deadly desires appear to put an end to the Jewish line, God has another plan. In His timing, God sets His plans in motion. The enemies of the Jews are defeated; a jubilant joy replaces their dread and despair.

A Firm Faith

Read Esther 9:1-32

While I cannot fully grasp the desperate situation that Esther faces, I can testify I have walked very close to the razor-sharp edge her story relays .When he was 17-years old and a senior in high school, our younger son, Dawson, faced a health crisis. A gifted athlete in top form, this handsome young man was the picture of health. Little did we know that a rare reaction to a viral infection soon would threaten his health and endanger his life. For a year Dawson underwent a series of tests and took many medications to try to curtail the devastating effects of the disease. When nothing seemed to work, we were faced with the bleak possibility of a life cut short. Casting ourselves on the Lord, Craig and I spent endless hours in prayer and fasting as we sought the face of our God and begged for the life of our son.

In the Christian life we refer to these times as *Gethsemane experiences.* Gethsemane is a place of abject desperation and desolation. This dark night of the soul is the time in which you find yourself shut up to the Lord. No one can rescue you or comfort you. You are left with no other option than to cast yourself on the Lord Jesus Christ. The anguish causes you to writhe in pain and cry out to God and say, *"If You are willing, remove this cup from Me, yet not My will, but Yours be done"* (Luke 22:42). The road to the cross passes through the Garden of Gethsemane. For the child of God, arriving at the end of yourself and dying to your plans is the agony of Calvary. However, the end result is *resurrection power!* When God moves on your behalf and resolves the situation, the joy bells start ringing!

I hasten to say that God does not always resolve our situations in the way we desire or expect. His ways are infinitely higher than ours are. His purposes and plans often mystify our limited viewpoint, but God stands strong on our behalf. *God is our refuge and strength, a very present help in trouble* (Ps. 46:1). God will set things right, either in this life or the next. His divine plans will not be overturned. Hebrews 11:1 says, *Now faith is the assurance of things hoped for, the conviction of things not seen.* Learn to walk by faith and trust in the Lord.

After a year of agony with Dawson's health scare, he began to respond to a regime of medicines and received a clean bill of health. While we know that the Lord used the doctor's medical ability coupled with powerful prescriptions to heal Daws, we credit the Lord for restoring our son's robust health and sparing his life. Gethsemane. Crucifixion. Resurrection! Hallelujah! What a Savior!

**1. Read Psalm 30:1-12. On February 10, 1999 we received a good report from Dawson's doctor about some blood work he had done. On that day I read this psalm and in the margin of my Bible next to Psalm 30:11-12 made a note of the date. According to these verses what is the result of unrestrained joy?

The dark places of this life make the bright spots glorious. God is not interested in making you happy. He is interested in making you holy. This process, called sanctification, walks us through the valley of suffering and loss. Lessons learned in the valley are life lessons that are painfully learned and never forgotten.

Esther experiences the dark valley of impending death for herself, her beloved cousin, and her people. Now joy bells ring out the day of celebration and jubilation! *A holiday of feasting and rejoicing and sending portions of food to one another* (Esth. 9:22) is proclaimed. The Jews celebrate God's goodness. He has given them mastery over their enemies.

As heirs of God we have been given mastery over our enemies: the world, the flesh, and the devil. We appropriate our birthright by faith. As we study the Word and spend time in prayer, we gain intimate knowledge of God. We discover His holy standard; our desire to live by it increases. A holy discontent is stirred by His standard. We begin to desire obedience. At this point I hasten to add: avoid achieving obedience through natural willpower. The Holy Spirit will empower us as we walk by faith. Faith is obedience to the Word of God, dependence on the Spirit of God, and confidence in the Son of God. *Faith comes from hearing, and hearing by the word of Christ* (Rom. 10:17). A queen understands the importance of personal Bible study. It enables obedience. It increases faith.

God is a good God. He is the giver of good gifts. *Every good thing given and every perfect gift is from above coming down from the Father of lights, with whom there is no variation or shifting shadow* (Jas. 1:17). When we study the Word of God, our capacity to know Him is enlarged. Our sense of His presence is heightened. The more we study the Word of God, the better we will know Him. The better we know Him, the more we trust Him. The more we trust Him, the quicker we are to obey Him. Obedience leads to soul satisfaction. Soul satisfaction leads to gratefulness. A grateful heart produces unspeakable joy in Jesus.

**2. Read and meditate on Psalm 103:1-22. David praises God for all His glorious benefits. What benefits does David mention?

For what are you praising God?

God is so good to us. Develop an attitude of gratitude for all the wonderful grace gifts He lavishes on us in the Lord Jesus Christ. Celebrate the goodness of God!

A Divine Defender

Read Esther 9:1-32

Craig and I live in the middle of 10 acres in a rural area outside of Memphis, TN. Our home has a sunroom off our family room. A bank of windows and a set of French doors give us a panoramic view of our azaleas, dogwoods, and stand of pine trees. To avoid obstructing the view, I have never installed any window treatments in this room. To entice birds into our yard in spite of the three large dogs that share our home, we have hung birdfeeders at various heights so that we might enjoy watching the Fayette County wildlife.

This summer we have watched a phenomenon develop in one of our fine-feathered friends. For the last 12 weeks a female cardinal has repeatedly hit our sunroom window. All day, every day, as often as eight times in one hour, the bird has continually flown into the window. This bird incessantly repeats this bizarre behavior from early in the morning until late at night. While she does not seem to be injuring herself, I cannot believe that this activity could be good for her. I can only imagine the headache she is giving herself! Originally I thought some item in my sunroom was enticing her but, after rearranging the furniture, she continued her daily assault on my window. I tried stacking pillows in the window so she could not see her reflection, but to no avail. I even held up my cat to scare her. I thought the sight of her natural enemy might dissuade her self-destructive behavior! Nothing has helped; the poor bird is continuing her persistent attack of my window.

At this point, you are probably wondering what spiritual application I intend to draw from Miss Cardinal's erratic behavior. Stay with me; I do have one! Our deranged bird's actions hurt no one but herself and are totally unproductive. Her self-destructive bent reminds me of people who are filled with bitterness. Nursing grudges or brooding over injustices only serves to feed the unquenchable flames of revenge. These sad, delusional people continually bang their head against the wall—or the window in this case—with their continual rehearsals of the wrongs they have suffered. Their actions only hurt themselves and build walls of resentment and strongholds of hatred. Like acid that ultimately destroys the container that holds it, the caustic aspect of hatred will eventually consume and destroy the heart that harbors it.

Haman's edict goes into effect on the 13th day of the month of Adar. On that day the ene-mies of the Jews have authority to attack and destroy God's chosen people. That same day Mordecai's decree goes into effect. The Jews can defend themselves and kill their enemies.

The Jews are given the right to defend themselves and to inflict just punishment against any who attack them. The Jews also are given the right to claim any property that belongs to their enemies as spoils of war. Mordecai's edict includes the exact terms that Haman's decree previously has established. The Jews defend themselves but do not pillage their enemies. The Jews understand the intent of Mordecai's decree as governed by the ancient command of holy war against the Amalekites.

The rules of ancient holy war stipulate plunder is not to be taken. Profit is not the purpose of a holy war; the execution of God's wrath is. The Jewish population shows self-control and judicious restraint by refusing to *lay their hands on the plunder* (Esth. 9:10). *The Jews struck all their enemies with the sword* (Esth. 9:5), but they do not line their pockets with the plunder of their enemies.

The Jews do not turn liberty into license. They demonstrate self-control. The best synonym for this characteristic is *discipline*. Self-control is mastery over the base desires of our human nature. The fruit of the Holy Spirit is self-control. It reins us in. It checks our motives.

Self-control seems as though it would be easy for Christians to cultivate. Personal experience tells us that is not the case. Indwelling us is an entity known as *the flesh*. In Romans 7:18-19 Paul describes the flesh: *For I know that nothing good dwells in me, that is, in my flesh; for the willing is present in me, but the doing of the good is not. For the good that I want, I do not do, but I practice the very evil that I do not want.* Been there. Done that. Galatians 5:17 says, *For the flesh sets its desire against the Spirit, and the Spirit against the flesh; for these are in opposition to one another, so that you may not do the things that you please.* Guerrilla warfare between the flesh and the Spirit is raging with us.

Craig and I have a boxer puppy. Sadie is 10-months old and the pride of our household. I was attempting to walk her on a leash, a social skill she has not mastered. As I tried to rein her in, she pulled against me. A tug-of-war of sorts ensued. Suddenly a sound caught her attention; she lunged toward it. The force of her weight caught me off-guard and took me off my feet. Had I not reacted quickly and regained my balance, she would have raced toward the back corner of the property and dragged me face-first in the dirt behind her!

The flesh is amazingly like our boxer puppy. The flesh is driven by temptations that appeal to our base natures. If we do not constantly rein it in, it will take off and give way to sin. The flesh cannot be redeemed or reformed; it requires the power of the Holy Spirit to crucify it. The Jews show self-control. They do not plunder their enemies, though they have the right to do so.

Among those who despise the Jews are Haman's 10 sons. Where do you think they learn their intense hatred of the Jewish race? Prejudice is a learned response. Haman has taught his boys to despise the Hebrew people just as his parents have trained him in the ways of hate. His words of intolerance lodge in the hearts of those boys and bear the fruit of bigotry as they grow into men. On the appointed day of slaughter, these boys join the ranks of those who hate the Jews. They intend to annihilate the Jews according to their father's evil edict. Consumed with hate and nearly choking on the taste of bile produced by years of malevolence toward the Jews, the bloodthirsty boys charge into battle. They are intent on finishing the work their father has started.

Haman's hatred outlives him. His decree against the Jews gives legitimacy to racial profiling and ethnic cleansing. His death silences his prejudicial voice, but the effects of his wickedness remained. Haman's sons are greatly impacted by his influence. He passes down his racism to them.

As mothers, be mindful of the influence you wield in the lives of your children and your children's children. Your children most likely will pattern much of their adult lives after yours. Your lifestyle will greatly influence your children and affect your grandchildren. How is that for a scary thought?

As mothers, we exert authority and influence. Our authority will slowly diminish throughout the 20-year course of our active phase of mothering. It will end when our children launch into the adult world. Influence continues. Influence outlives us. For good or for evil, we are continually affecting our children through our influence. Haman influences his sons for evil. His evil outlives him. We can influence our children for godliness. Our passion for God can outlive us.

The Bible condemns any form of prejudice. David describes those who suffer from the malignancy of racism. Psalm 69:4 says, *Those who hate me without a cause are more than the hairs of my head; those who would destroy me are powerful, being wrongfully my enemies.* Racial intolerance of any kind is denounced in the Word of God.

**1.God categorizes people as either lost or saved. He makes room for no other distinction. Read Acts 10:34-35. What is God's standard?

We are compelled by Christ to view people based on their spiritual condition and not on their race, creed, or color. If they are children of God, we receive them as family members. If they are outside the family of God, we endeavor to build relationships to reach them with the gospel. Our failure to comply with God's standard of unconditional love is sin. Bigotry of any type condemns us to a life of bitterness and hatred toward any sect we have deemed unworthy. Like my confused cardinal, we will end up hurting ourselves with the endless bashing of our heads against the wall. How foolish to live such a life!

All who name the name of Jesus have been placed into the body of Christ and the family of God. Prejudice has no place in the Christian community. We are brothers and sisters in the Lord.

**2. Read Galatians 3:26-28. What does this passage teach us about the body of Christ?

We are one in the Lord. The Spirit of God produces harmony and unity.

3. Read 1 John 4:19-21. What insight can we learn from John's passage?

An attitude of love toward the brethren is evidence of genuine conversion. God's love is shed abroad in our hearts by the indwelling Holy Spirit. To harbor prejudice against those outside the faith is unacceptable; to tolerate bigotry toward those within the family of God is unthinkable. *We love, because He first loved us* (1 John 4:19). In John 13:35 Jesus says, "*By this all men will know that you are My disciples, if you have love for one another.*" Love is our Christian hallmark.

Haman's legacy to his sons is hatred and prejudice. A queen leaves a legacy of love for others and a passion for the things of the Lord.

Weekly Summary

Please record insights gleaned from this week's study.

An Enormous Enemy

Read Esther 9: 1-32

Five hundred men and the 10 sons of Haman are killed in the citadel in Susa. When the king discovers the incredibly high numbers of those who oppose the Jews, he wonders aloud, *"What then have they done in the rest of the king's provinces!"* The king is stunned at the enormity of the enemies of the Jews. God has always had (and will always have) His enemies. Satan is behind all of them. Satan is skillfully manipulating those who do not know God. The devil has always had (and continues to have) legions of God-haters.

In the Garden of Eden God pronounces judgment on Satan. In Genesis 3:15 God says, *"I will put enmity between you and the woman, and between your seed and her seed; He shall bruise you on the head, and you shall bruise him on the heel."* Contained within that verdict is the first prophetic reference to the Messiah. *The seed of the woman* refers to the virgin birth of Jesus. At Calvary Satan will bruise Him on the heel. The Lord's resurrection from the dead will crush Satan's head and seal his fate.

Satan's plan always has been to interrupt the Jewish lineage of the Messiah. If he could prevent the birth of Jesus, he would retain the title deed of humanity Adam surrenders in the garden. The fact Adam and Eve are so easily deluded must give Satan hope. Even after God's divine judgment, Satan continues to attempt to disrupt God's plan.

Throughout history see Satan's fiendish fingerprints as he attempts to maneuver people to carry out his schemes. Satan turns the heart of Pharaoh against God's chosen people. Their arrival at the Promised Land reveals scores of enemies determined to resist the Jews. Herod, motivated by Satan, slays all the male children 2 years of age and under in Bethlehem to try to kill the Lord Jesus. Judas is Satan's pawn. Pilate, Herod, and the religious rulers of Jesus' day are held hostage by the prince of darkness to do his will. Hitler is used in Satan's vain attempt to wipe out God's chosen people. Time and again the enemy orchestrates elaborate schemes against the Jewish race, but God's hidden hand of providence has prevailed.

Satan continues to attempt to destroy the Jews. Now, in the church age, he levels his arsenal against the church. Our adversary, *the devil, prowls around like a roaring lion, seeking someone to devour* (1 Pet. 5: 8). Satan knows he is a defeated foe. He hopes you never discover this truth. He knows he will spend eternity in hell. Knowing his ultimate end, he has set about to delude as many as possible. They will join him and his minions in the lake of fire.

Hell is a place *where their worm does not die, and the fire is not quenched* (Mark 9:44). Hell is prepared for Satan and his demons. It is not created for humankind. God *desires all men to be saved and to come to the knowledge of the truth* (1 Tim. 2:4). Jesus offers to all the free gift of salvation. However, the shed blood of Jesus only applies to the sin debt of those who receive Him by faith. Any who die outside a personal relationship with Christ are cast into the lake of fire. For all eternity they will be in the company of Satan and his demons.

1. Read Revelation 20:10-15. At the end of the age, what will happen to Satan?

_____

Who will join him in a Christless eternity?

_____

Beloved, God's will is for all to be saved and none to be lost. John 3:16-17 Jesus says, *"For God so loved the world, that He gave His only begotten Son, that whoever believes in Him shall not perish, but have eternal life. For God did not send the Son into the world to judge the world, but that the world might be saved through Him."* God has made a way of escape, but not everyone will accept it. Those who refuse the free gift of salvation will be kept under Satan's sway and ultimately cast into the lake of fire to endure eternal judgment.

Satan has always had people willing to do his bidding. King Ahasuerus learns that many of these inhabit his kingdom. He asks Esther if she has a further request. Esther says, *"If it pleases the king, let tomorrow also be granted to the Jews who are in Susa to do according to the edict of today; and let Haman's ten sons be hanged on the gallows."* Esther wants an additional day to rid the country of those who despise the Jews and intend to do them harm.

Esther also asks the king to hang Haman's 10 dead sons on the gallows as a warning to those who would continue to cling to prejudice or bigotry. Swift judgment against a crime and capital punishment serve as a deterrent against further crimes against the crown. Ecclesiastes 8:11 says, *Because the sentence against an evil deed is not executed quickly, therefore the hearts of the sons of men among them are given fully to do evil.* Esther requires swift and public retribution against the enemies of the state.

The change in the king's attitude toward Esther is noteworthy. Not only does he grant her first petition, he now asks for her advice and follows her counsel. God grants her grace in the king's sight. King Ahasuerus approves Esther's request. A second day is added to the edict to allow the Jews *to defend their lives and rid themselves of their enemies* (Esth. 9:16).

The Jews who were in Susa assembled also on the fourteenth day of the month Adar and killed three hundred men in Susa, but they did not lay their hands on the plunder. Now the rest of the Jews who were in the king's provinces assembled, to defend their lives and rid themselves of their enemies, and kill 75,000 of those who hated them; but they did not lay their hands on the plunder (Esth. 9:9-16).The Jews are free to retaliate against the proposed genocide of their enemies. However, they hold back and do not profit from their enemies.

Satan entices us to sin with temptations that appeal to *the lust of the flesh and the lust of the eyes and the boastful pride of life* (1 John 2:16). The Jews wisely resist the temptation to take Satan's treasure.

**2. Joshua leads the people against Jericho. God declares the city and all its inhabitants are to be destroyed, with the exception of Rahab and her family. He has given Joshua very specific instructions about the possession. Read Joshua 6:17-19. What are Joshua's instructions about the possessions of the inhabitants of Jericho?

_____

Read Joshua 7:1. What happens?

_____

Joshua sends a small contingent of soldiers to take Ai. This should have been a small skirmish and an expected victory for the Jews. The men of Ai put the Israelites to flight. Joshua goes before the Lord. He is stunned by this defeat on the heels of the supernatural victory over Jericho. Read Joshua 7:10-15. What does God say to Joshua?

_____

Joshua sends for the tribes. Read Joshua 7:16-26. Achan is discovered to have stolen some of the enemies' plunder. What has he taken?

_____

What is the penalty for his sin?

_____

God will not allow His people to profit from their enemies' plunder. Beloved mom, do not lust after the enemies' treasure. Learn to be content with what God provides. Paul writes, *Not that I speak from want, for I have learned to be content in whatever circumstances I am. I know how to get along with humble means, and I also know how to live in prosperity; in any and every circumstance I have learned the secret of being filled and going hungry, both of having abundance and suffering need* (Phil. 4:11-12).

We have an enormous enemy. Satan has legions of well-trained demons. He is constantly assaulting our minds and tempting our flesh. That's the bad news. When we saturate our souls with the Word of God and surrender our wills to His Spirit, we can stand against the wiles of the devil. Paul writes, *But in all these we overwhelmingly conquer through Him who loved us. For I am convinced that neither death, nor life, nor angels, nor principalities, nor things present, nor things to come, nor powers, nor height, nor depth, nor any other created thing, will be able to separate us from the love of God, which is in Christ Jesus our Lord* (Rom. 8:37-39). That's the good news! We have an enormous enemy, but we have an even greater God. Through Jesus Christ we are more than conquerors.

A Commemoration Celebration

Read Esther 9:1-32

The joy bells are ringing in Susa and the surrounding provinces. The Jews have destroyed their enemies. God has intervened and stopped the impending genocide of His people. *Then Mordecai recorded these events, and he sent letters to all the Jews who were in all the provinces of King Ahasuerus, both near and far, obliging them to celebrate the fourteenth day of the month Adar, and the fifteenth day of the same month, annually* (Esth. 9:20-21).

**1. Read Esther 9:22. How do the Jews celebrate God's goodness to them?

_____

God has overruled Satan's demonically inspired plan. Satan's scheme to disrupt the Jewish lineage of Christ is overturned. A celebration of unspeakable joy ensues! Joy, *inexpressible and full of glory* (1 Pet. 1:8), is one of the distinguishing marks of a Christian. Indescribable joy is the byproduct of a genuine conversion and is the birthmark of a child of God. It defies logic and ignores circumstances. It rises above the downward pull of our sin-cursed society. It transcends pain and heartache. In John 15:11 Jesus says, *"These things I have spoken to you, so that My joy may be in you, and that your joy may be made full."* Unfathomable, unspeakable, and incomprehensible joy is ours in abundance.

Joy is *available* to every child of God, but it is not automatic. Like so many of the grace gifts tied to our salvation, joy is appropriated by faith. No matter what the circumstances are, we do not have to lose our joy. We may choose to lose it, but the joy of Jesus is the birthright of every blood-bought child of God. Joy is an outward manifestation of a heart that is fixed on Him. Psalm 32:11 says, *Be glad in the Lord and rejoice, you righteous ones; and shout for joy, all you who are upright in heart.* First Chronicles 16:27 says, *Splendor and majesty are before Him, strength and joy are in His place.* Job 8:21 says, *He will yet fill your mouth with laughter and your lips with shouting.* Lift up your head, child of God, and rejoice in the Lord!

**2. Jesus is the source of genuine joy. Read Psalm 16:11. What does this passage say about the joy of the Lord?

_____

How do you maintain this joy?

When we walk with the Lord in unbroken communion and fellowship, He gives us His joy without measure. The loss of our joy is an indication that because of sin, we have broken fellowship with the Lord. A spiritual checkup is necessary to uncover the sin. Repentance and confession will restore the joy of the Lord and fill our soul with singing.

The world can experience happiness but not genuine joy. Happiness depends on situations, circumstances, and conditions. Joy, however, is not dictated by situations, nor is it determined by circumstances or affected by conditions. Joy is rooted in a living relationship with the Lord of Glory. Because of Jesus we are able to overcome our natural disposition toward despair in the face of difficulty. We can walk through suffering and sorrow with joy in our hearts. Only the child of God can know sorrow and joy in equal measure at the same time. The joy of Jesus ensures our contentment regardless of our circumstances.

Craig and I consider being a part of the royal family of God a privilege . We have had many opportunities to celebrate seasons of joy with precious Christian friends. We have lingered over many meals and shared the goodness of the Lord with our forever friends. I had always assumed potluck meals were a product of our culture; it appears it was a well-known practice in Esther's day, too. The tradition of *sending portions of food to one another* (Esth. 9:22) is obviously appropriate for times of celebration.

The captors have perpetrated unspeakable suffering on the Jews. Now the enemies are vanquished. The time has arrived to rejoice in God's providence and power on their behalf.

When Haman determines the date to carry out his plot to exterminate the Jews, he uses an ancient custom of casting lots. A lot is called *Pur*. The plural form of this word is *Purim*. *When it came to the king's attention, he commanded by letter that his wicked scheme which he had devised against the Jews, should return on his own head and he and his sons should be hanged on the gallows* (Esth. 9:25). To commemorate God's sovereign preservation of the Jewish nation, a day of celebration is declared. *Therefore they called these days Purim after the name of Pur. And because of the instructions in this letter, both what they had seen in this regard and what had happened to them, the Jews established and made a custom for themselves and for their descendants and for all those who allied themselves with them, so that they would not fail to celebrate these two days according to their regulation and according to their appointed time annually. So these days were to be remembered and celebrated throughout every generation, every family, every province and every city; and these days of Purim were not to fail from among the Jews, or their memory fade from their descendants* (Esth. 9:26-28). The Feast of Purim was established to celebrate God's goodness. To this day the Jews still celebrate Purim.

Esther and her people have great reason to rejoice. Sorrow has been turned into gladness and mourning has turned into a holiday (Esth. 9:22). Operation Celebration is under way!

A Righteous Recollection

Read Esther 9:1-32

The little Book of Esther, tucked in the pages of the Old Testament, is unique in many ways. Perhaps the most noteworthy is the fact the name of God is not mentioned. As we have studied the book, we can readily testify to the obvious, albeit invisible, presence of God. God is always at work, although often we are unaware of His divine methods. Spending time with Him awakens our spirit to His presence—at least in part. In 1 Corinthians 13:12 Paul writes, *For now we see in a mirror dimly, but then face to face; now I know in part, but then I shall know fully just as I also have been fully known.* Our limited vision of God does not constrain Him. One day in the future we will know Him as fully as He knows us now!

I have only one hobby—photography. When Jason was a junior in high school, he served on the yearbook staff. He borrowed a school camera and was given black-and-white film with instructions to snap random pictures of high-school students and functions. Although I had always taken many pictures, his borrowed camera intrigued me. A new love of photography was born. A new camera, with all the bells and whistles, ensued. Noting my obvious love of photography, several friends have suggested that I take some courses on the subject. However, my joy is much more about recording the people that I love rather than the art of photography.

Another aspect of this hobby quickly followed to manage and organize the massive number of pictures that I continually take. Scrapbooking my family memories has become a natural outgrowth of my obsession with pictures. In the process I have discovered my real passion is acting as the family historian and protecting our precious memories. I love holding a copy of my memory in my hand and not just in my heart. While some people journal their lives, I photojournal mine! This has become an expensive and time-consuming hobby; I am not telling anyone to invest in it as I have. But I will say that I treasure the reams of pages that contain the essence of a life well-lived in service to the Lord and to my family. Nothing delights me more than to revisit, through the archives of our scrapbooks, the wonderful memories of our family times together.

My disclaimer is this: I did not start this hobby until Jason was a high-school senior. Before that season in my life, I took a lot of pictures and stored them in photo-safe boxes. With two small children hanging on me, attempting to scrapbook my photos would have been out of the question! I did not have the time nor the money to invest in this hobby. However, I am so grateful for the countless pictures of my boys that I have taken throughout the years and the treasured memories that they represent. Busy mom, my advice to you is to take many pictures of your children. You are unaware of how quickly they are changing; you will treasure these memories. You may never want to scrapbook them or display them. That may not be your interest. I am not suggesting that scrapbooking is required of a godly woman. But at least give yourself that option by taking lots of pictures. Label them and file them safely away to await a season in your life when time is not at such a premium.

I value memories. The fleeting years combined with the high rate of speed with which we all live often causes memories to fade rapidly and drift into the vanishing recollections of the past. Pictures are a sure way of recalling the past and relishing sweet family moments and priceless memories.

1. Journaling is another wonderful way to record the hallmarks of your walk with God. Reread Esther 9:20. What does Mordecai do after the dramatic events that lead to the preservation of the Jews?

God has moved on behalf of the children of Israel. Jewish history has been altered because of the events the Book of Esther records. Mordecai records these events for posterity. From generation to generation he wants the story of God's providential care to be remembered and celebrated. Esther 9:29-31 says, *Then Queen Esther, daughter of Abihail, with Mordecai the Jew, wrote with full authority to confirm this second letter about Purim. He sent letters to all the Jews, to the 127 provinces of the kingdom of Ahasuerus, namely, words of peace and truth, to establish these days of Purim at their appointed times, just as Mordecai the Jew and Queen Esther had established for them, and just as they had established for themselves and for their descendants with instructions for their times of fasting and their lamentations.* If this official celebration of Purim had not been established, the oral tradition of this event might have been lost.

The command of Esther established these customs for Purim, and it was written in the book (Esth. 9:32). As moms we can use national holidays to teach our children the events that are vital to our nation's history. These can become great learning opportunities.

Use Christian celebrations to teach your children about our faith. Make sure your celebration of Christmas is centered around the birth of our Savior. As our boys grew up, we had all the trappings of this holiday, but we kept the birth of Christ at the center of our celebration. Easter is a another glorious time to celebrate. The world makes this holiday about bunnies, bonnets, and baskets. Moms, use Easter to teach the lesson of the empty tomb. Use Christian books and DVD's to help communicate the truths these holidays commemorate.

**2.Read Deuteronomy 6:4-9. (Keep your place in Deuteronomy, because we will return to it.) This is one of the most concise passages on the best way to influence your children with your values and your faith. What does this passage say?

_____

How can you incorporate this insight into your parenting skills?

_____

_____

_____

Family devotionals can be very meaningful to your children. However, sharing the value of your faith as you go about your day is the best way to instill your Christian values. When a child is reared in a loving environment where Jesus Christ is Lord, he/she is very likely to receive Jesus Christ at an early age. Let your children see the reality of Christ in you. The impact of your faith lived before them is immeasurable.

**3. Read Deuteronomy 6:17-25. From this passage what parenting insight can you gain?

_____

_____

In what practical ways can this passage impact your mothering techniques?

_____

_____

Use your children's natural curiosity to teach them spiritual truths. Use events, anniversaries, traditions, holidays, and celebrations to tell them about our great God. The Jews built memorials to instruct future generations. We can build monuments of our faith through journals or photographs or celebrations. We can share the goodness of the Lord with our children and future generations. Living like a queen in the present requires of good recall of the past!

A Humble Heart

Read Esther 10:1-3

And so the story of Esther concludes. *Now King Ahasuerus laid a tribute on the land and on the coastlands of the sea* (Esth. 10:1). This appears to be a reference to the king's power. His subjects pay him tribute. The accomplishments of King Ahasuerus are recorded in the *Book of the Chronicles of the Kings of Media and Persia.* The inclusion of this fact in Scripture reminds us, lest any doubt, that supporting literary works validate these events.

The Book of Esther ends with a fitting tribute to Mordecai. He is *great among the Jews, and in favor with the multitude of his kinsmen, one who sought the good of his people and one who spoke for the welfare of his whole nation* (Esth. 10:3). Mordecai is promoted to a position second only to that of King Ahasuerus. He has earned a reputation for being a fair and impartial head of state. Perhaps the most incredible line of Mordecai's résumé is the fact that he is a Jew. As exiles, the Jews are alive and living in Persia by permission of a Gentile government. They could have been killed when their homeland was conquered. For a Jew to be promoted to a position of authority would have been unheard of were it not for grace. God divinely and sovereignly places Esther and Mordecai in powerful positions within the palace so that His purposes and plans might be fulfilled.

Esther and Mordecai are people of character. We assume that in Mordecai's home Esther learned the importance of godliness. Throughout her story she demonstrates grace and dignity. Esther's quiet confidence in God crowns her life with strength and humility.

Although I have lived in Memphis all my life, I never have witnessed anything like the storm that blew through the Bluff City in 2003. As the storm ravaged the city, it knocked down power lines and toppled enormous trees. Property damage was estimated in the millions of dollars. As I drove throughout midtown Memphis, arguably one of the worst-hit sections of town, I was saddened to see massive trees splintered and uprooted. In many cases a tree obviously was diseased. Although undetectable when the tree was standing, decay was eating away at the heartwood. The tree appeared healthy on the outside and was still experiencing seasonal leaf cycles. Yet hidden deep inside were disease and decay, which were steadily weakening the ecosystem of the tree and slowly destroying it. Although the tree appeared to be healthy, it was dying. The high winds only hastened its inevitable end.

I could not help but think of the spiritual parallel between the diseased trees and human nature. Outward appearances can be very deceiving. Many people appear to be Christians. They may profess to belong to the Lord and may have church affiliations. They may conform their outward behavior to adhere to a strict code of ethics. All the while, their hearts are diseased. Jeremiah 17:9 says, *The heart is more deceitful than all else and is desperately sick; who can understand it?* If the heart is wicked, in only a matter of time its true identity is revealed. No matter how grandiose the outward appearance, no matter how self-righteous the life, no matter how liberal the giving, no matter how many religious rituals are faithfully maintained, a person outside of a personal relationship with Jesus Christ is spiritually dead and headed toward eternity in hell. Regardless of their outward appearances or the façade they carefully maintain, they are dead on the inside. In time this will be revealed. Like the mighty trees that fell, great will be their destruction.

**1. This truth is best described in a parable Jesus told in Luke 18:9-14. After you read this passage, in your own words describe the story. From this parable what can you learn about hypocrites and pride?

Contrary to popular opinion, character does matter. True Christian character is a byproduct of your salvation. Esther is a wonderful example of a godly woman who demonstrates strength and dignity. Faced with a crisis, she fasts and prays. Following Mordecai's godly counsel she approaches the king without an invitation and changes the course of Jewish history. When she speaks to the king, she shows great restraint and allows God to speak through her. She uses reverent restraint to plead her case and diplomatic eloquence to identify her enemy. In all these instances Esther displays humility and grace.

Humility is an attitude of the heart rather than an action. It has been described as freedom from pride and arrogance—a modest estimate of one's own worth. In spiritual terms humility is a true perception of our unworthiness apart from the saving grace of Jesus Christ. A humble heart recognizes that genuine value is found in belonging to Jesus. I am of value and worth because of Jesus; apart from Him I can do nothing (John 15:5). Humility springs from a true assessment of self based on the Word of God. Luke 14:11 says, *For everyone who exalts himself shall be humbled, and he who humbles himself shall be exalted.* We are most like our Lord than when we are humble of heart.

**2. Obviously Christ is the ultimate example of humility. His capacity to lay aside all the glories of heaven in order to take on Himself the form of a man is the purest depiction of humility. Read Philippians 2:3-11. Write down your insight on this valuable character quality.

How can we develop this godly quality in our lives?

How can we teach it to our children?

Peter writes, *And all of you, clothe yourselves with humility toward one another, for God is opposed to the proud, but gives grace to the humble* (1 Pet. 5:5). Develop a humble heart; in due time let God exalt you.

Likely Esther learns humility from Mordecai. We can assume he consistently models it as she is reared in his home. He certainly possesses this rare quality. The concluding verse of the Book of Esther confirms Mordecai's gentle and contrite spirit. A Jew, highly exalted in a Gentile court, manages to be not only great among his own people but also well spoken of by his kinsmen. He seeks the good of his people and looks after the welfare of the nation. God highly exalts Mordecai. Proverbs 22:29 says, *Do you see a man skilled in his work? He will stand before kings; he will not stand before obscure men.*

Our God continues to amaze us. His purposes and plans are so much higher than ours. We can scarcely dare to dream of the things He has in store for those who love Him. Jeremiah 29:11 says, *"For I know the plans that I have for you," declares the Lord, "plans for welfare and not for calamity to give you a future and a hope."* God knows what He is about in our lives. Our part is to be a useable vessel in the hand of the King. Ephesians 3:20 says He is *able to do far more abundantly beyond all that we ask or think, according to the power that works within us.* Hallelujah! What a Savior!

The Book of Esther has many valuable truths. I'll quickly recap the story. God elevates an unknown, orphaned girl to the Persian throne. He moves in the heart of a stubborn, unbelieving Gentile king. He turns the tables on a wicked, anti-Semitic official and captures Haman in his own net. He destroys the enemies of the Jews. He highly exalts a humble Jewish man to the right hand of the king of Persia. God not only does the unexpected, He also upholds the unassuming with His strong right hand.

Beloved mom, God is faithful and true. Through the Lord Jesus Christ He desires to have a personal relationship with you. God has a purpose and a plan for your life. Like Esther, He desires to display the reality of Christ in your life. He wants to fellowship with you now in the present and to spend eternity with you in the future. As we have been learning in our study of Esther, God moves invisibly. Yet, He is invincible. He is in the process of bringing His sovereign plan to fruition.

Through the study of the Book of Esther you have learned how to live like a queen. Your conversion experience places you into the royal lineage of Jesus Christ. We are heirs of God and joint-heirs of Jesus. We have learned to rest in God's goodness and trust in His faithfulness. His ways may seem illogical, His timing may seem unfathomable and His delays may feel unbearable, but His grace and mercy are undeniable.

God is good! Hallelujah! What a Savior!

A Faithful Finish

Read Esther 10:1-3

The story of Esther has all the makings of a great tale. A casual read reveals a villain, a damsel in distress, a hero, a surprise twist, and a happy ending. A closer look uncovers the true meaning behind the story. The Book of Esther is the story of God's sovereignty. He elevates an orphan to the throne. He uses her to change the course of Jewish history. God's hand moves silently but diligently. He brings His divine plan to pass.

As in Esther's day, God is intimately acquainted with the details of our lives. Convinced we wield control over our circumstances, we expend untold effort and energy to keep the pace dictated by schedules and routines. We often assume God is not involved in the mundane. We are convinced God is not interested in the monotony of mothering.

Faith-walking is required to see God at work in the mediocrity of daily living. Learning to live in God's sovereignty is the lifelong pursuit of every child of God. I pray that the study of Esther has opened your eyes of understanding. Make a habit of looking for the handprint of the Father in your daily life. Spend time in prayer. Make the study of God's Word a part of your daily routine. The study of the Word will sensitize you to the quiet stirrings of the Father.

**1. Psalm 119 is an ode to the riches of the Word of God. Read Psalm 119:1-8. Whom does God constantly bless?

_____

How can we walk in the ways of the Lord?

_____

Salvation is a gift. Sanctification is a process. What can we do to increase the productivity of His work in our lives?

_____

We have finished our study, but we have not finished the pursuit of God. Esther is placed in the palace *for such a time as this*. God has put each of us in the place He has specifically and divinely designed. He can use the many missteps we take to bring us to this season of life. He has overcome our stubbornness and rebellion. In Romans 3:25-26 Paul writes, *This was to demonstrate His righteousness, because in the forbearance of God He passed over the sins previously committed; for the demonstration, I say, of His righteousness at the present time, so that He would be just and the justifier of the one who has faith in Jesus.* His hand has been in every event that has happened in our lives. He has had a plan to bring us to this place *for such a time as this.* God wants us to live like members of His monarchy. He wants us to live up to our royal potential. He waits for us to stake claim to our royal residency. He desires for us to reign in real life! We are heirs of God and joint-heirs with Jesus. Now let's learn to live like we are!

Weekly Summary

Please record insights gleaned from this week's study.

_____

_____

_____

_____

_____

_____

_____

_____

_____

_____

_____

_____

_____

_____

_____

_____

_____

_____

_____

_____

_____

_____

Appendix

How to Become a Christian

Dear one, have you ever had a time in which you have given your heart to the Lord? Do you have the assurance that if you were to die right now, you would go straight to heaven to spend all eternity in the presence of the Lord Jesus Christ and all His followers? If not, please let me share with you how you can be saved.

Admit Your Sin

First, understand that you are a sinner. The Bible says, *All have sinned and fall short of the glory of God* (Rom. 3:23). In Romans 6:23 the Bible says, *For the wages of sin is death*. That means that sin has separated us from a Holy God. We are under the sentence of eternal death and separation from God.

Abandon Self-Effort

Secondly, you understand that you cannot save yourself by your own efforts. The Bible is very clear that it is *not by works of righteousness which we have done, but according to His mercy He saved us* (Titus 3:5). Again, in Ephesians 2:8-9 the Bible says, *For by grace you have been saved through faith; and that not of yourselves, it is the gift of God; not as a result of works, that no one should boast.*

Acknowledge Christ's Payment

Thirdly, believe that Jesus Christ, the Son of God, died for your sins. The Bible says, *God demonstrates His own love toward us, in that while we were yet sinners, Christ died for us* (Rom. 5:8). That means He died a sacrificial death in your place. Your sin debt has been paid by the blood of Jesus Christ, which cleanses us from all sin (1 John 1:7).

Accept Him as Savior

Fourthly, put your faith in Jesus Christ and Him alone for your salvation. The blood of Christ does you no good until you receive Him by faith. The Bible says, *Believe on the Lord Jesus Christ, and you shall be saved* (Acts 16:31).

Have you had a time in your life that you have taken this all-important step of faith? If not, I urge you to do it right now. Jesus Christ is the only way to heaven. He says, "*I am the way, the truth, and the life; no man comes unto the Father, but by Me*" (John 14:16).

Would you like to become a Christian? Would you like to invite Jesus Christ to enter your heart today? Read over this prayer. If it expresses the desire of your heart, you may ask Him into your heart to take away your sin, fill you with His Spirit, and take you home to heaven when you die. If this is your intention, pray this prayer.

"Oh, God, I'm a sinner. I am lost and I need to be saved. I know I cannot save myself, so right now, once and for all, I trust You to save me. Come into my heart, forgive my sin, and

make me Your child. I give you my life. I will live for You as You give me Your strength. Amen."

If you will make this your heartfelt prayer, God will hear and save you! Jesus has promised that He will never leave nor forsake anyone who approaches Him in faith. In John 6:37 He says, *"The One who comes to Me I will certainly not cast out."*

Welcome to the family!

The Disciplines of Devotion

I must discipline myself:

- To make time to be with the Lord

- To quiet myself before Him

- To harness my mind and focus on Him

- To spend time in praise and worship

- To pray effectively for my assigned prayer burdens

- To pray fervently for my husband and children

- To cover those who have been lent to me in prayer

- To meditate on and pray back Scripture to the Lord

- To study the Word of God—reading, re-reading, and meditating on it

- To dig into the Word of God. I will mine it for nuggets of gold that I can build into my life and incorporate into my Christian experience.

- To apply myself to living out the truths of the Word

- To walk in the Spirit

- To crucify the flesh daily—even moment to moment if necessary

- To place myself under godly preachers and teachers to instruct me and build me up for the ministry God has given me

- To spend time with like-minded people to challenge and encourage my walk in the Lord

- To be well-pleasing to my Heavenly Father

- To pursue personal holiness on a daily basis

- To impact my world—my sphere of influence with the reality of Jesus Christ

Blessed Unbeliever

Many a Christian woman finds herself in a marriage with an unbeliever. Perhaps when you married, you both were lost. Then after you were married, you got saved; now you are unequally yoked to an unbeliever. Or perhaps before you married, your husband represented himself as a child of God, but now his lifestyle evidences that he has never entered into a personal relationship with Jesus Christ. What does the Bible say?

Please understand that if you are a child of God and you are married to an unbeliever, certain things in your marriage will be more difficult. However, God has a plan; He will give you the grace to be victorious. He intends to use you to impact your unbelieving husband for the kingdom of God.

First Peter 3:1-4 says, *In the same way,* (referring to the previous passage about Christ being our example) *you wives, be submissive to your own husbands so that even if any of them are disobedient to the word,* (either an unbeliever or a carnal Christian) *they may be won without a word by the behavior of their wives, as they observe your chaste and respectful behavior. And let not your adornment be merely external—braiding the hair and wearing gold jewelry, or putting on dresses; but let it be the hidden person of the heart with the imperishable quality of a gentle and quiet spirit, which is precious in the sight of God* (parentheses mine).

This passage teaches that a godly wife can win her husband to Christ—without nagging, preaching, complaining, or threatening—merely by living a godly and righteous life before him. When a godly woman chooses to respond *in the same way* as Christ did *(and while being reviled, He did not revile in return; while suffering, He uttered no threats, but kept entrusting Himself to Him who judges righteously),* she can be used of the Lord to reach her husband. However, if she chooses to attempt to coerce him into a personal relationship with Christ, she ties God's hands in the matter. God will have to work in her life until she can trust Him fully with the spiritual condition of her husband before He is free to work in the husband's life. If you are married to an unbeliever, God's mandate to you is to develop personal holiness in your own life and to free God to work in your mate's life.

In his letter to the Corinthian church Paul addresses this situation. In the early church quite commonly one spouse became a believer in Christ while the other did not make a commitment to Him. Members look to Paul for counsel on this matter. Paul writes, *And a woman who has an unbelieving husband, and he consents to live with her, let her not send her husband away.* In other words, this is certainly not grounds for divorce. He goes on, *For the unbelieving husband is sanctified through his wife, and the unbelieving wife is sanctified through her believing husband; for otherwise your children are unclean, but now they are holy* (I Cor. 7:14). Being married to a believing spouse does not make an unbeliever saved. Nor are the children automatically saved; that is not what he teaches here. What he is saying is that when at least one spouse is saved, a greater chance exists that the unbelieving spouse and the children will enter a saving knowledge of Jesus Christ than if they were in a home without any believers present. Furthermore, the blessing of God is on the life of the believing spouse; all in the household will benefit from that. *For how do you know, O wife, whether you will save your husband? Or how do you know, O husband, whether you will save your wife?* (1 Cor. 7:16) You, dear mom, may be God's chosen instrument to lead your husband and your children to a saving knowledge of Jesus Christ! However, wait patiently; trust the timing to the Lord. Meanwhile, develop personal holiness in your own life.

As you wait on God, develop personal holiness in your own life through Bible study and prayer. Ask God to give you verses that you can claim for your spouse's salvation. Develop your ability to be a fervent prayer warrior on behalf of your mate. You might want to pray for your spouse 1 Timothy 2:3-4, *This is good and acceptable in the sight of God our Savior, who desires all men to be saved and to come to the knowledge of the truth*. Personalize that passage and pray it (and others like it) for your spouse (and your unsaved children).

Marriage, in and of itself, is not easy. Constantly work to keep it in good repair. Demanding schedules, family needs, financial responsibilities, and busy lifestyles pull us in all directions. This makes us fight for quality time together. Being married to an unbeliever has some additional built-in issues for you to tackle, but, beloved mom, God can give you the power and the strength to reach your husband for the Lord Jesus Christ. May you be found faithful to the task! Hallelujah! What a Savior!

A Study in the Strategy of Satan

The Bible teaches that when you and I become followers of Jesus Christ God Himself supernaturally delivers us out of the domain of darkness and transfers us into the kingdom of His dear Son. Ephesians 2:1 states that through the new birth He has made alive (spiritually) those of us who were formerly dead in trespasses and sins and who walked according to *the prince of the power of the air,* the spirit who now works in the sons of disobedience (unbelievers). A very real spiritual being named Satan exists. He is the enemy of our souls. Although he has lost the spiritual battle for your eternal soul, he continues to harass you in an attempt to render you ineffective in your spiritual pilgrimage on earth on your way to heaven.

Seeing how the Scripture speaks of Satan is helpful. To see just a few of the names he is given and to learn something of his character, look at the following Scriptures:

In Job 2:1-13 we see that he is the *accuser of the brethren.*

In John 8:44 he is *a murderer from the beginning, and does not stand in the truth, because there is no truth in him. Whenever he speaks a lie, he speaks from his own nature; for he is a liar, and the father of lies.*

In Matthew 4:1 and I Thessalonians 3:5 we see he is *the tempter.*

In Matthew 13:19 he is *the evil one.*

John 10:10 he is known as *the thief (who) comes only to steal and kill and destroy.*

Second Corinthians 4:4 states that Satan is *the god of this world.*

Colossians 1:13 says he is the *ruler of the domain of darkness.*

Understanding all these facts, what are you and I as believers to do? Again, look to the Scriptures for instruction and admonition.

First Peter 5:8-9 says, *Be of sober spirit, be on the alert. Your adversary, the devil, prowls about like a roaring lion, seeking someone to devour.*

James 4:7 urges, *Submit therefore to God. Resist the devil and he will flee from you.*

First Peter 1:13 says, *Gird your minds for action, keep sober in spirit, fix your hope completely on the grace to be brought to you at the revelation of Jesus Christ.*

Ephesians 6:11-18 (perhaps the definitive passage on spiritual warfare) teaches us that we should *put on the full armor of God, that we might be able to stand against the schemes of the devil . . . take up the shield of faith with which you can extinguish all the flaming arrows of the evil one.*

Second Corinthians 2:11 says, *We are not ignorant of his schemes* (his methods or systematic processes of attack).

Ephesians 4:27 says, *Do not give the devil an opportunity* (that is a foothold in your life or mind). Resist his attacks with your renewed mind. Protect yourself from the onslaught of the wicked one by casting down every stronghold. Second Corinthians 10:3-5 says, *For though we walk in the flesh, we do not war according to the flesh, for the weapons of our warfare are not of the flesh, but divinely powerful for the destruction of fortresses. We are destroying speculations and every lofty thing raised up against the knowledge of God, and we are taking every thought captive to the obedience of Christ.*

Finally we can take comfort in realizing, *the battle is not yours but God's* (2 Chron. 20:15) and *greater is He that is in you than he that is in the world* (1 John 4:4).

The enemy is strong and his power should not be underestimated. However, our God is immensely more powerful. Satan is a defeated foe! Stand firm in the Lord!

Scripture Memorization

1. Jesus says, "*You are the salt of the earth; but if the salt has become tasteless, how can it be made salty again? It is no longer good for anything, except to be thrown out and trampled under foot by men*" (Matt. 5:13).

2. Jesus says, "*You are the light of the world. A city set on a hill cannot be hidden; nor does anyone light a lamp and put it under a basket, but on the lampstand, and it gives light to all who are in the house. Let your light shine before men in such a way that they may see your good works, and glorify your Father who is in heaven*" (Matt. 5:14-16).

3. Jesus says, "*Do not store up for yourselves treasures on earth, where moth and rust destroy, and where thieves break in and steal. But store up for yourselves treasures in heaven, where neither moth nor rust destroys, and where thieves do not break in or steal; for where your treasure is, there your heart will be also*" (Matt. 6:19-21).

4. Jesus says, "*For this reason I say to you, do not be worried about your life, as to what you will eat or what you will drink; nor for your body, as to what you will put on. Is not life more than food, and the body more than clothing? Look at the birds of the air, that they do not sow, nor reap nor gather into barns, and yet your heavenly Father feeds them. Are you not worth much more than they? And who of you by being worried can add a single hour to his life?*" (Matt. 6:25-27).

5. Jesus says, "*And why are you worried about clothing? Observe how the lilies of the field grow; they do not toil nor do they spin, yet I say to you that not even Solomon in all his glory clothed himself like one of these. But if God so clothes the grass of the field, which is alive today and tomorrow is thrown into the furnace, will He not much more clothe you? You of little faith!*" (Matt. 6:28-30).

6. Jesus says, "*But seek first His kingdom and His righteousness, and all these things will be added to you. So do not worry about tomorrow; for tomorrow will care for itself. Each day has enough trouble of its own*" (Matt. 6:33-34).

7. Jesus says, "*Behold, I send you out as sheep in the midst of wolves; so be shrewd as serpents and innocent as doves*" (Matt. 10:16).

8. Jesus says, "*And whoever in the name of a disciple gives to one of these little ones even a cup of cold water to drink, truly I say to you, he shall not lose his reward*" (Matt. 10:42).

9. Jesus says, "*Come to Me, all who are weary and heavy-laden, and I will give you rest. Take my yoke upon you and learn from Me, for I am gentle and humble in heart, and YOU WILL FIND REST FOR YOUR SOULS. For My yoke is easy and My burden in light*" (Matt. 11:28-30).

10. And Jesus came up and spoke to them, saying, "*All authority has been given to me in heaven and on earth. Go therefore and make disciples of all the nations, baptizing them in the name of the Father and the Son, and the Holy Spirit, teaching them to observe all I have commanded you; and lo, I am with you always, even to the end of the age*" (Matt. 28:18-20).

Leader Guide

Leader Guide

This study can be effectively utilized in a group setting which facilitates interaction and accountability. You may obtain DVD-format videos to enhance and expand the potential impact of the study. (For ordering information see the resource page in the back of the book.) This Leader Guide offers helpful hints to incorporate the study into a Women's Ministry setting.

Introduction

Live Like a Queen is an in-depth, 10-week Bible study from the life of Esther. The goal of the study is to teach moms how to take the profound truths of the Word of God and make them practical in their daily lives.

Leader Qualifications

The heart of a servant is required for you to be a faithful leader. The ideal leader has a committed walk with the Lord to assist members in their pilgrims' progress. Your goal as a leader is not to teach the material but rather to act as a facilitator to help the members glean truth from the Word of God and to apply it.

How to Begin a Group

1. Pray. Get the heart of the Father before you attempt to begin any new work for the Lord. This study is designed for group participation in a church or home setting, but it also will work for individual use. Ask the Lord to guide to the group those He would have participate.

2. Respectfully seek approval. Make the proper appeal to the leadership of the church to incorporate this study into the church's overall program.

3. Enlist and train leaders. One leader with one or two assistants per group lessens the work load and ultimately grows new leaders.

4. Promote the study. Since the program is designed for moms, the nursery and children's ministry of your church will provide a built-in audience. Your church may have a Young Married Department which also may give you ample opportunities to promote the Bible study. You can do this either by written invitation or in the form of announcements. Anywhere moms are found, you will have an outreach opportunity. Because of the nature of this program, unchurched or unsaved moms will be intrigued and interested. Virtually every mom, whether or not she knows the Lord, wants to be a good mother. This study naturally will introduce those outside the faith to the things of the Lord. For those inside the body of Christ it offers a wealth of training and truth.

5. Address childcare. Since this study is written for moms, the issue of childcare is paramount. If possible, offer childcare on site. If this is not available, try to suggest other options.

6. Set a schedule. Allow at least two hours a week for the group session to get the maximum benefit from each week's study. Spend 45 minutes in small-group discussion; allot one

hour for the group to see the video in a large-group session. Provide for a short break in-between.

7. Open registration. After approximating the number of participants you anticipate, order written materials and the set of 10 DVD's. Obtain ordering information at *www.jeanstockdale.com* or *www.hannibalbooks.com*. Allow six weeks before the starting date to complete this process and to insure all materials are in hand.

8. Divide the participants into small groups. To promote the maximum amount of sharing, arrange the moms into groups of about 12 to 15 women. Grouping the moms according to the age range of their children (for instance, by newborn, preschool, school-age, teens) will facilitate the sharing and the opportunities to meet needs. Ask leaders to contact each group member one week before the first session to introduce the leadership team, assign room numbers, and answer any questions.

How to Train Small-Group Leaders

1. Gather your leadership for one meeting. Invite all of your leaders to a meeting in a home or at the church several weeks before you will begin the program. This will be the only meeting necessary to adequately train your leaders and assistants.

2. Review the workbook. Walk the leaders through the various sections of the study. Encourage them to familiarize themselves with the workbook. Show them the format. Questions are to be answered five days out of each week.

3. Instruct them. Advise leaders to be in the room a few minutes before their groups are expected. Set up the chairs in a circle and be ready to greet the small-group members. Start on time. Open in prayer and address prayer requests, but watch the time. Allow five to 10 minutes for prayer time and then get to the homework. Discuss the homework. In the discussion time, the leader and her assistants benefit from being overly prepared and very familiar with the homework. This way they can easily guide the discussion and cover the material. Time constraints may cause the leader to have to move quickly through some of the questions to work her way through all five days of homework. Skipping a question or two is left up to the leader's discretion and may be dictated by the time. Ask each leader to highlight any question she especially wants to cover. Leaders can formulate one concise truth to sum up the week's study and end on that note. Instruct leaders to close in prayer and to dismiss on time.

4. Get them to start doing the study. Ask leaders to begin doing the study. Advise them to stay about a week ahead of their group at all times. This will allow leaders to be comfortable with any questions that might arise and will aid in their discussion.

5. Get them excited. The group leader sets the tone of the small group. If leaders are excited about what they are learning, their group members will follow suit. If leaders are doing their homework and are arriving prepared, this will challenge the group members to be faithful as well.

6. Get them involved. Ask your small-group leaders and assistants to contact their members as often as possible. Advise them to use cards, phone calls, and emails to keep their moms enthusiastic about the program.

7. Urge the leaders to become prayer warriors. Encourage the leaders and assistants each week to be prayed up and prepared.

How to Lead a Small Group

1. Who can lead or assist in a small group? Any growing Christian mom can lead a small group. The ideal leaders and assistants have vibrant testimonies of the saving grace of the Lord Jesus Christ, are actively involved in the church program, are given to prayer, and are committed to becoming students of the Word of God. The purpose of the small-group leader and/or assistant is to facilitate the discussion. Ideally the small-group leader will be just a bit further down the road of mothering than are the group members she is leading. The moms attending are looking for caring, considerate leadership from a mom who is passionately pursuing personal holiness and practical righteousness in her own home and who is willing to bring others along in the process.

2. What qualities do you seek in a small-group leader? She is a woman of godly character who can guide the conversation and guard the privacy of the women involved in the group. Confidentiality is non-negotiable. At the first small-group session, the leader ideally will ask members to commit to confidentiality; ask members to pledge to keep within the group what is shared.

3. What are some good leadership traits? A good leader has good people-skills as well as a good working knowledge of the Word of God. Here are some specific suggestions:

• Maintain good eye contact. Use good body language that expresses openness and acceptance.

• Develop the discipline of listening as well as the ability to speak the truth in love.

• While you lead the group, learn to silently pray without ceasing.

• Do not allow one group member to dominate the conversation or to distract the group from the Bible study. If someone attempts to take over the conversation, try to redirect the discussion. Perhaps you can say, "Thank you for your insight. Can some one else add to her comment?" Assistants can be very helpful to direct the conversation, especially if someone becomes long-winded or gets off the subject.

• Do not allow error to be espoused, but be careful not to quench the spirit of the woman who needs to be carefully and gently corrected.

• Do not fear silence. If you ask a question and no one answers immediately, as leader simply sit quietly and wait until a volunteer offers an answer. Most of the time, if you are patient, a volunteer will emerge. You may need to rephrase the question to stimulate a response.

• Do not call on anyone to answer a question or to lead in prayer. Understand that some in your group may never speak up or answer a question. Our goal is not to teach women to talk; our goal is to lead moms to study the Word of God and to glean truth. Consider asking for a volunteer to offer to lead in prayer rather than calling on someone.

• Encourage your leaders to phone, email, or write notes to their small-group members. Encourage members' involvement and affirm their efforts.

• The purpose of the small group is to study the Bible. Open and close each session with prayer offered either by the leader or assistant. Prayer requests can be shared, but ask the members to be brief and to the point. Some groups ask their members to write on an index card the need. Before the session ends distribute these cards among the group to be sure someone, outside of class, lifts the request to the Lord. Valuable discussion time can be lost in reciting or rehearsing the details of innumerable prayer requests. While these needs are valid and deserve adequate attention in prayer, this Bible study is not the proper place for an extended prayer meeting. Our goal is to instruct through the Word of God and to encourage by the Spirit of God. Gently guide the prayer time to a limit of about five to seven minutes maximum to provide ample remaining time for group discussion.

4. What are some small-group guidelines? Begin and end on time. From the beginning establish good habits for the small group. Remember, we are training moms to train godly children. If you cannot keep your word about the structure and format of your program, how can you expect a mom to learn to keep her word to her children? Be a good steward of your time. Start the group on time, even if all members have not arrived.

5. How is the room arranged for small-group study? Sitting in a circle creates an intimate atmosphere in which to share. Ask your assistant to sit across from you to help facilitate the natural flow of sharing. Be careful that no one is left to sit outside the circle. Draw in late-arrivers and include them.

6. What is the goal of each small-group session? Open in prayer to set the tone of the session. Begin to review and discuss each week's questions. Since you probably will not have time to go over every question the homework asked, highlight one or two key questions or phrases from each day's homework that you, from your own study, believe are the most important issues to address. All answers likely will be obvious as members complete their daily homework assignments. However, make sure you have finished each question in your own work so that you are prepared to deal with or correct any misconceptions. As leader be prepared to share from your own experience, so members will see you as a fellow struggler rather than as someone who "has it made" in the parenting arena. Limit your own sharing to about 45 seconds per answer, so members will get the idea that their sharing needs to be in summary form rather than stream-of-conscience rambling. The goal is to help our moms make the bridge between profound truth and practical application.

How to Facilitate the Large-Group Study

1. What is a good room arrangement for the lecture DVD?
   Position the television monitor so all the members can see. Placing the chairs in rows is usually the most effective arrangement and allows any late-arrivers to slip in without disrupting the group. Leaders, invite your small-group members to sit together during the lecture time to develop friendships and promote fellowship among the members.

2. What is a good format for the lecture portion of this ministry?
   Select an administrator. She will be responsible for registration, enlisting, and training leadership, dividing small groups, and starting the DVD presentation. She will welcome the moms, open in prayer, and begin the lecture portion on DVD. She will become the face of this ministry, so carefully and prayerfully consider how you fill this leadership position.

3. What is the most important part of this ministry to moms?
   Prayer. Without a doubt, to be effective this ministry must be born out of prayer and be soaked in prayer. Our intention is to give God the liberty to work in and through the leadership to impact and influence the participants with the Word of God.

A Summary of the Sessions

Week 1

All the participants will attend a general session during what will become small-group time, since registration typically continues up to this point. Having a registration area set up for any who previously have not filled out the necessary paperwork is helpful. Direct all the moms into the lecture hall.

- The administrator will open this session with prayer.
- The administrator will begin by introducing herself and her leadership team, which is made up of small-group leaders and assistants.
- Books will be handed out if necessary. Participants can purchase books at the time of registration.
- The Bible study can be explained.
- Although the study is self-explanatory, the administrator can use this time to walk the participants through the Bible study.
- The study consists of weekly studies that include five daily readings and questions. The preschool moms are required to answer only the questions that feature the double set of asterisks (**) for discussion in the small group but are encouraged to answer all the homework.
- Moms who do not finish the homework are strongly encouraged to attend and participate.
- Video 1 will be viewed.

Week 2 through Week 9

Small groups will meet to discuss the study. They will begin with week one and continue through week 8 of the homework. After 45 minutes of small-group discussion, the group will be dismissed to the lecture hall, with a 15-minute break provided between the small-group and large-group meetings. During the large-group time participants will view week 2 through week 9 of the DVD's. The lectures are deliberately designed to stand alone as individual messages and not simply to rehash the material the moms have just studied and then discussed.

Week 10

Have the whole group meet together for Share Day. During the time typically allotted for small-group discussion, allow the moms to share in the large-group setting what God has taught them through the study of the life of Esther. Finish with a prayer of thanksgiving to the Lord for the work He has accomplished. View final DVD number 10.

Additional Resources

Congratulations and God bless you for completing the study on the life of Esther. Jean's prayer is that you have learned how to reign in your everyday life in God's Kingdom!

Jean has additional Bible studies available. They are similar in design and format as *Live Like a Queen* and will encourage and challenge you and your friends to apply practical Bible truths with life changing results.

For ordering information on resource materials you may
- Visit Jean Stockdale's website at: *www.jeanstockdale.com*
- Email Jean at *jean@standingnearthecross.com*
- Call 1-877-409-5564 and leave your contact information.

Proverbs and Principles for Parenting Practically Perfect Progeny

Filled with tidbits of truth and words of wisdom, Proverbs gives us a wonderful plan of parenting and addresses the most practical needs for daily living.

This book is excellent for an individual or a group Bible study. You may obtain DVD's or CD's to enhance and expand the potential impact of the study. The 196-page workbook is structured for a seven-week personal study or 10 weeks with accompanying DVD's. Each week contains five daily lessons with thought-provoking questions for the reader to answer. The study can be effectively utilized in a group setting which facilitates interaction and accountability. The Leader Guide, included in the workbook, offers helpful hints to incorporate the study into your church program.

Run Well, Finish Strong

Through the study of 2 Timothy, you will discover how to pass a living faith along to the next generation and learn how to impact and influence your children to choose Jesus Christ.

This book is excellent for an individual or a group Bible study. You may obtain DVD's or CD's to enhance and expand the potential impact of the study. This 219-page workbook is structured for an eight-week personal study or 10 weeks with accompanying DVD's. Each week contains five daily lessons that contain thought-provoking questions for the reader to answer. The study can be effectively utilized in a group setting which facilitates interaction and accountability. The Leader Guide, included in the workbook, offers helpful hints to incorporate the study into a church setting.

Mirror, Mirror on the Wall

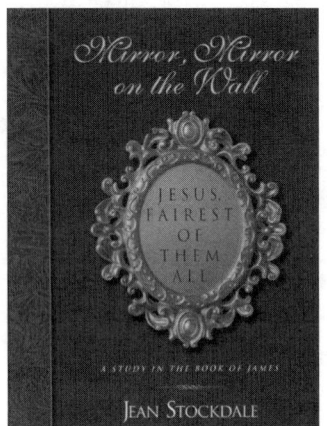

James instructs believers to look intently into the perfect law of liberty and to abide in God's truth. Our study will teach you how to deal with anger, how to respond to testing, and how to choose your words carefully. You will learn how to develop the fine art of Christian mothering by looking into the mirror of God's Word. Look and see what areas of your life need to be conformed to the image of Jesus Christ.

This book is excellent for an individual or a group Bible study. You may obtain DVD's or CD's to enhance and expand the potential impact of the study. This 219-page interactive workbook is structured for a eight-week personal study or 10 weeks with accompanying DVD's. The self-guided study contains five daily lessons per week. The study can be effectively utilized in a group setting for the added benefit of discipleship and accountability. The Leader Guide, included in the workbook, offers helpful hints to incorporate the study into a church setting.

The Secret Source of Strength

This stimulating study examines the life of Elijah and shows moms how they, modeling their lives after the Old Testament character Elijah, can have fresh fire to encourage them and draw them closer to God. The study of the Old Testament prophet reveals that God can work in the life of a common person. It can strengthen any mom for the sometimes arduous journey she faces in parenting.

This book is excellent for an individual or a group Bible study. You may obtain DVD's or CD's to enhance and expand the potential impact of the study. This 170-page interactive workbook is structured for a eight-week personal study or 10 weeks with accompanying DVD's. The self-guided study contains five daily lessons per week. The study can be effectively utilized in a group setting for the added benefit of discipleship and accountability. The Leader Guide, included in the workbook, offers helpful hints to incorporate the study into a church setting.